PREPARING CEOs

FOR SUCCESS

"What I Wish I Knew"

This book offers the collective wisdom of over two dozen of America's top CEOs. The participating CEOs pictured overleaf have contributed their insights from experience totaling hundreds of years in diverse, innovative enterprises.

The authors—and the participating CEOs—hope you profit from the wisdom and experience that proudly rest between the covers of this book!

The Participating CEOs

Brad Anderson
Former Vice Chairman & CEO
(Retired 2009)
Best Buy Company, Inc.

Stephen A. Furbacher
Former COO
(Retired 2008)
Dynegy, Inc.

Riley P. Bechtel*
Chairman & CEO
Bechtel Corporation

John H. Hammergren
Chairman, President, & CEO
McKesson Corporation

Alan L. Boeckmann
Chairman & CEO
Fluor Corporation

H. Edward Hanway
Former Chairman & CEO
(Retired 2009)
CIGNA Corporation

Richard T. Clark
Chairman, President, & CEO
Merck & Co., Inc.

Susan M. Ivey
Chairman, President, & CEO
Reynolds American, Inc.

Cristóbal I. Conde
Chairman & CEO
SunGard Data Systems, Inc.

William R. Johnson
Chairman, President, & CEO
H.J. Heinz Company

Peter A. Darbee
Chairman, President, & CEO
PG&E Corporation

Donald R. Knauss
Chairman & CEO
The Clorox Company

John V. Faraci
Chairman, President, & CEO
International Paper Company

Kenneth D. Lewis
*Former Chairman,
President, & CEO*
(Retired 2009)
Bank of America Corporation

Indra K. Nooyi
Chairman & CEO
PepsiCo, Inc.

David N. Weidman
Chairman & CEO
Celanese Corporation

David J. O'Reilly
Former Chairman & CEO
(Retired 2009)
Chevron Corporation

William Weldon
Chairman & CEO
Johnson & Johnson

James W. Owens
Chairman & CEO
(Retiring 2010)
Caterpillar, Inc.

Geoff Wild
President & CEO
Cascade Microtech, Inc.

Ronald A. Rittenmeyer
Former Chairman,
President, & CEO
(Retired 2008)
EDS Corporation

Patricia Ann Woertz
Chairman, President, & CEO
Archer Daniels Midland Co.

Dennis Sadlowski
President & CEO
Siemens Energy
& Automation, Inc.

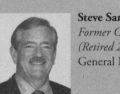

Steve Sanger
Former Chairman
(Retired 2008)
General Mills Corporation

In addition to the contributions from those
presented here, perspectives are included
from two CEOs who requested to remain
anonymous.

* Photos are included at the discretion
of each CEO.

Randall L. Stephenson
Chairman, CEO, & President
AT&T Inc.

PREPARING CEOs FOR SUCCESS

"What I Wish I Knew"

CEO Study Sponsored by

William R. Johnson
Chairman, President, & CEO
H.J. Heinz Company

Lead Researchers and Authors

Leslie W. Braksick, Ph.D.
James S. Hillgren, Ph.D.
The Continuous Learning Group, Inc. (CLG)

For permission to use any portion of this book, or obtain a copy of the CEO Study findings, please visit www.clg.com/publications/ceostudy.aspx or contact CEO Study, CLG, 500 Cherrington Parkway—Suite 350, Pittsburgh, PA 15108, 412-269-7240 x 2038, ceostudy@clg.com.

Library of Congress Cataloging-in-Publication Data
Braksick, Leslie W.
Hillgren, James S.
Preparing CEOs for Success: *"What I Wish I Knew"*
ISBN-13: 978-0-692-00790-7
1. Chief Executive Officer (CEO)
2. Leadership
3. Management
Book design: Scattaregia Design
First edition published 2010 by H.J. Heinz Company, Pittsburgh, PA.
Printed in the United States of America

10 9 8 7 6 5 4 3 2 1

DEDICATION

Preparing CEOs for Success
is dedicated to every new CEO
and to every leader
who aspires to become one.

CONTENTS

FOREWORD

Developing and preparing future CEOs is one of corporate America's most important and challenging obligations. It is an obligation Heinz takes very seriously. However, as I reviewed the many excellent books and articles on the subject of CEO succession, it became quite clear that what was missing was the unvarnished perspective from sitting CEOs themselves. Therefore I undertook this study to capture and leverage the experiences of current Chief Executives on how best to develop and prepare future CEOs.

The input collected by Dr. Leslie W. Braksick and Dr. James S. Hillgren of CLG was outstanding. It will be clear to you after reading even the first few pages that each CEO spoke honestly and openly about "what I wish I knew" before he or she got the job. I am grateful to the other CEOs who participated in the study for their candor. Their insights inform the sections on CEO prerequisites and should be invaluable to companies focused on CEO succession.

Being appointed CEO of a global Fortune 500 company is a great honor, privilege, and responsibility. It reflects a tremendous vote of confidence in an individual's ability to lead, manage, and grow an organization. With that honor comes the expectation that we will earn that trust and respect, every single day. I hope this book reminds sitting and future CEOs of the things we each need to do well—and those things we can help others do well, in preparation for their time at the helm. It is our collective responsibility to create successors who will generate sustained value for all our stakeholders, including our shareholders, employees, customers, and communities.

— William R. Johnson
Chairman, President, & CEO
H.J. Heinz Company
May, 2010

How Did This Book Come About?

This book emerged from a need to more widely disseminate the findings of some important research on "what CEOs wished they knew" before they got the job.

The project was sponsored by CEO Bill Johnson of the H.J. Heinz Company, in support of his own CEO succession planning and development efforts. The work was made possible by the participation and remarkable candor of Bill and 26 other sitting CEOs of global companies. The research was conducted by Drs. Leslie W. Braksick and James S. Hillgren of CLG during 2008–2009.

After we shared the study's lengthy formal report with the participating CEOs and companies, others quickly heard about the study and wanted to learn from its findings, too. It became clear that more copies of the study were needed and that a handy book-format presentation of the study's findings would be tremendously valuable. Thus, with the agreement of the participating CEOs, we have released the report as the book you are reading. Now more leaders at all levels—and aspiring CEOs—can learn from some of the most successful CEOs of our time.

The first three parts of the full report appear in their entirety in this book, with no change in content. The fourth part from the full report presents detailed profiles of the participating companies, CEOs, and their career progressions. For this book, we greatly condensed this portion.

This book offers hundreds of valuable quotations from our participating CEOs. However, we have intentionally not attributed quotes to specific individuals. The purpose of our research, and of this book, is to provide unvarnished advice—based on the real experience of sitting CEOs—for the advancement of preparing future CEOs and executives. Often, our participants' experiences were unflattering for themselves or their companies, and yet they shared openly and honestly with the assurance of confidentiality at an individual level. With our bar set high for CEOs whom we invited to participate in the study (minimum of $6B in revenue; running a global company), it matters not who said what, but rather that an impressive collection of CEO peers offered these important insights for future peer CEOs.

How This Book Is Organized

Part I   **What We Discovered**

Summarizes study findings in eight key themes, featuring very candid and thoughtful quotes by the participating CEOs in response to the question: *"What do you wish you knew prior to becoming CEO?"*

Part II   **The CEO Prerequisites**

Presents information on the personal qualities and attributes, career experiences, and managerial practices to which CEOs attributed their success. Rich in information helpful to profiling successful CEOs—who they are, what they have done, and how they lead. Also provides concrete focus to those accountable for developing future CEOs: Boards of Directors, Board Chairmen, Board HR and Succession committee members, sitting CEOs, and heads of HR.

Part III   **The CEO Handbook**

Eight chapters of advice from the CEOs to their successors and others who aspire to be CEOs of global, multibillion-dollar companies. Presents answers to: *"What advice do you have for your successor… or others who might aspire to be CEO of a global company like yours?"* This part is essentially a CEO Handbook of advice by these top global leaders, presented in eight topical areas. Includes all interview quotes gleaned from the study, grouped by topic without attribution to specific participants.

Presented as eight mini-reports so it can be easily read and referenced as part of a company's senior executive development processes. Includes recommendations by the authors to give leaders and aspiring CEOs a starter set of concrete suggestions and next steps for immediate action.

Part IV   **Participating CEOs**

Profiles of the CEOs and their companies.

What We
PART I # Discovered

AUTHOR
Leslie W. Braksick, Ph.D.
The Continuous Learning Group, Inc. (CLG)

ONE

WHAT LED
TO THE STUDY?

The tenure of CEOs has never been shorter. Turnover of CEOs globally in 2008 reached 14.4%, with a slight decline in North America. The 2009 recession slowed turnover a bit, but by year's end CEO turnover was displaying an uptick. More than one-third of all CEO turnover (globally) was performance-based. As a result, CEO success and CEO succession are foremost concerns of Boards and major investors. Over the past decade, this topic also has become a favorite of business magazines, journals, and books.

Questions around how to groom and prepare an executive to be a successful CEO are ones that every business school faculty member, management consultant, and Wall Street analyst would feel well qualified to weigh in on. However, there is one voice underrepresented in the debate —that of sitting CEOs. In particular, what is missing is what sitting CEOs wished they had known before they moved into their new role, what they felt underprepared for, and what surprised them. This vantage point is critical to the design of successful CEO preparation and development strategies.

William R. Johnson, Chairman, President, and CEO of H.J. Heinz Company, and Steve Clark, his Chief People Officer, recognized this gap in the planning for CEO succession and decided to do something about it. In response, Johnson has sponsored a study inviting sitting CEOs of select global companies to provide their perspectives on several key areas.

Participating CEOs were asked to respond to the following questions:

1. **What was the state of the company when you became CEO?**
2. **What do you wish you had known prior to coming into the job as CEO?**
3. **What were the things you felt least prepared to handle?**

4. **What things that were important to the job did you find yourself best able to handle?**

5. **What things outside of the work setting best prepared you for this job?**

6. **What surprised you the most about the CEO role?**

7. **What would you want your successor to know if you were mentoring him/her?**

Johnson asked his longtime consulting partner, CLG's Leslie Braksick, Ph.D., to conduct the study and to report back the findings in a way that would be helpful to the Boards, CEOs, and senior HR professionals involved in CEO succession matters, as well as to current and emerging CEO candidates.

"It is important to me that we learn from the experiences of sitting CEOs and share them with the future generation of leaders. I wanted to provide a venue where they could speak openly, honestly, and confidentially about what they wish they knew before getting into the job—so we could help future CEOs to be even better prepared for these challenging roles. Being CEO of a global corporation is an honor and a privilege. The lives and futures of many people are entrusted to you. For this reason, it is of the utmost importance that we better understand how to help CEOs to be highly successful early in their tenure."

William R. Johnson, *Chairman, President, & CEO*
H. J. Heinz Company

Braksick enlisted the help of her colleague, CLG's Jim Hillgren, Ph.D., and they conducted 27 CEO interviews. Each of the interviews took approximately one hour. Fourteen interviews were conducted face-to-face in the CEO's office, while 13 interviews were conducted by phone. Together with CLG partner Tracy Thurkow, Ph.D., and Jennifer Howard, they analyzed the interview comments and prepared these findings and recommendations.

TWO

WHO PARTICIPATED:
PROFILES IN COURAGE

Twenty-seven CEOs participated in this study. The majority were from companies with workforces of more than 10,000 people and revenues of $4B or greater. A profile of each CEO, his/her company, and his/her career progression to the CEO position is in Section 4 of this Report.

- There were twenty-four men and three women.

- Twenty-four rose through the ranks of their companies in ascending to the CEO position, while three CEOs who participated in this study were recruited from the outside directly into the CEO position. No significant differences in the reported experiences emerged between those who rose in the ranks versus those who came in from the outside.

- Twenty-three of the CEOs inherited companies that were historically and currently performing well from a financial perspective. The other four companies were entering, in the midst of, or just emerging from turbulent times. The majority of the CEOs reported that while the company was strong financially, significant shifts in strategies and/or business models were needed in order to be competitive in the future.

- All but one of the participating companies were headquartered in the United States.

THREE

THE BIG EIGHT THEMES

In all of the interviews, each CEO outlined the business challenges he/she faced going into the job. All were faced with significant challenges stemming from the business climate, the need to change their company's existing portfolio of products or services, a shifting global marketplace that drove the need to change asset allocation or how their company was structured, or the state in which their predecessor had left the business.

Each CEO objectively described the challenging business conditions they faced beginning on day one. However, 100% of those interviewed reported that those business challenges—though significant—were, and are not, the hardest part of the job. They felt well-prepared to deal with them.

The CEOs had many prior jobs, challenges, and learning experiences that prepared them well to lead their businesses through high growth, downsizing, strategic repositioning, etc. While the business circumstances they faced required their greatest leadership skills to navigate, they felt well-equipped to do this.

On the other hand, there were eight common themes that emerged in the interviews—things CEOs said that they were not prepared for and things that the CEOs wished they knew before moving to the role. These eight themes were:

1. **Tenacity, Patience, and Judgment Required for Decision Making**
2. **Unique Challenges Posed by the Leadership Team You Inherit**
3. **Prioritization Takes on a Whole New Meaning**
4. **Developing a Trusting Relationship With Your Board is Essential**
5. **Transitioning Well Matters**
6. **Unending Governance Challenges**
7. **Public Scrutiny: No Private Life**
8. **Isolation of the Job**

1. Tenacity, Patience, and Judgment Required for Decision-Making

One "surprise" that the CEOs frequently mentioned was how few decisions they actually made. Unlike their previous roles as business unit or group presidents, in which they had full P&L or business portfolio responsibilities, the CEOs reflected on the fact that they really only make three to four big decisions in a given year, the impact of which is not seen for months or even years. In addition, we heard several speak of the need for tremendous courage, tenacity, and judgment when making these key strategy-impacting decisions, often with management or the Board split on which direction to take. The weightiness of the decisions made at this level, combined with the reported lack of people with whom to have an open and candid dialogue about sensitive issues, only compounded the pressure they felt and underscored the need for courage, judgment, and resolve.

> *"... The crisis state post-9/11 forced me into a mode of fast learning and evaluating so I could make wise decisions ASAP."*

Additionally, many CEOs spoke of the lag time in decision implementation and the importance for repetition in communicating decisions and the rationales behind the decisions long after the need to communicate should have passed.

"I was least prepared for making a few decisions with such big consequences."

"I was least prepared for the in-depth knowledge of the balance sheet that I needed to have. 9/11 increased the urgency for me to learn about the balance sheet, and I had to do it fast. The crisis state post-9/11 forced me into a mode of fast learning and evaluating so I could make wise decisions ASAP."

"I had to learn quickly that I was no longer really 'in control.' I could not effectively control the decisions and actions of the company. I had to enable my staff to make decisions and learn how to effectively influence them since I could no longer control the decisions that were being made."

"You cannot lead a business you don't understand. Understanding of your business, honesty, and a commitment to lead the company well are the keys to being a great CEO."

"I was not prepared for the fact that the CEO makes only three to four major decisions a year that have big impact. These decisions need to be made with confidence."

"The role of CEO is both the most and the least powerful job in the company. As CEO, I am charged with managing and leading the enterprise, but at the same time, I am subject to review and criticism by numerous 'bosses.' Furthermore, I frequently lack objective, real-time data to determine whether what I want done or what I expect to be done is actually getting done."

"I believe that having the courage of conviction for great executive leadership to go down difficult roads when necessary requires deep-seated values and fundamental confidence in one's own capabilities, well-balanced by restraint of ego."

The CEO must have a great deal of stamina and resolve. The person must be able to take multiple "blows" and setbacks, and still come back for more. This includes mental and physical stamina and resolve.

2. Unique Challenges Posed by the Leadership Team You Inherit

Much was shared by the CEOs during the interviews about issues with the leadership teams they inherited. In many cases, they were leading former peers, some of whom also had been candidates for the CEO job. Several expressed frustration with performance issues that their predecessor had not addressed—performance issues that, in some cases, consumed disproportionate time, energy, and attention of the new CEOs over several months, even years, thereby delaying the introduction of much needed changes in strategy. The CEOs spoke with passion about the challenge of balancing their own and the organization's needs for leaders with content expertise and institutional knowledge/history and leaders who share and represent their vision and values. The challenge of aligning and leading a new leadership team was the second most commonly mentioned "what-I-wish-I-knew."

"I think a big challenge of the CEO role is addressing people issues promptly and decisively. If you are not going to face and deal with the people issues, you have no business saying 'yes' to the job of CEO."

"As CEO, I was encouraging people to do things differently. It took a long time for my team to get on board with me. My biggest supporters today were my biggest opponents back then."

"I was surprised by the high degree of fear and mistrust. I was also surprised by how long it took to bring old and new members of my leadership team together. I had so much to do around communication."

"Overnight I found myself managing peers, all of whom stayed. They all held on at first. I was so much younger than all of the people I was managing. I wish I had coaching on how to manage former peers. Suddenly, all relationships changed once I received the promotion to the CEO position."

"As COO, I dealt with tangible and measurable issues. As CEO, I quickly learned that I must act dispassionately and objectively in my relationships with people and that I must make decisions about people and about business units that potentially conflict with my old 'loyalties.'"

"I learned the difficult task of dealing with an incumbent leader that I had grown up with during my career in the organization and who was not what the business needed. He had even been my boss previously. Four years into my tenure, I replaced him . . . and I should have done it years earlier."

"Perhaps one of my earliest, if not biggest, surprises was in the whole area of the depth of management and leadership talent. It would have been helpful to me if I had had a better assessment of the individuals on the senior management team at the time I assumed the role of CEO. I was surprised that members of the team were weaker than I had assumed, and, consequently, I inherited underperformers. Because I was not initially aware of some of these weaknesses, it took awhile (approximately two years) to assess and realign the team and, hence, delayed the implementation of some significant changes in strategy and execution that I believed important to our future."

"I joined a solid and respected senior team. My hope was that this team would stick with me. Many of them had been candidates for my job (CEO). I worked hard to get to know them. I spent a significant part of my first 90 days looking, listening, and learning from them."

"I think a big challenge of the CEO role is addressing people issues promptly and decisively. If you are not going to face and deal with the people issues, you have no business saying 'yes' to the job of CEO."

"I began working with the leadership team to break down the silos and make it in everyone's interest to have everyone succeed, not just individual divisions; we were going to become 'one company.' I had a few people on the team who just did not get this; they did not accept how we were going to change. In a couple of cases, this was really disappointing because they were talented people and we were friends."

"When I became CEO, I knew that we had to make some radical changes in our organization, our processes, and how we thought about the business, and, in particular, our culture. I knew it was going to take time. What surprised me was that our mid-management and front-line employees knew this and were ready to change—in fact, they were anxious to change. However, our senior management did not see the need. I had to spend more time with senior management, repeating the message. They just did not get it. The higher I went up the organization, the less insight there was into issues."

"I believe there is a form of acute senior executive disease which I have come to call 'top warp.' Top warp distorts a senior executive's perspective and information by reason of structural, cultural, and behavioral forces at the top of his/her organization. They insulate and isolate the senior executive from the workforce, the company's customers and key suppliers, and those below him/her in the organization. Top warp is best prevented by vaccination with great basic values and having and using great feedback means. Most horrible leadership fatalities are heavily contributed to, if not caused by, top warp. Most of my big mistakes were caused in large part by letting top warp get the better of my CEO balance."

"Collaboratively shaping the senior leadership team is critical because CEO succession is really executive suite succession."

"We all support each other closely here at this company. It's part of the business culture here, and it's important to us all."

"I had not had a lot of previous M&A experience. I had a new team at the top of the organization resulting from a merger, where I did not know eight out of the top ten folks in the new company. It took a lot longer to bring them together than I ever imagined it could have."

"During the three years prior to becoming CEO, my predecessor and I worked closely in reviewing all of our key executive talent. As the time neared for me to move into the role, my predecessor began addressing many of the talent and style issues. Where appropriate, he helped them exit with grace and dignity. In the meantime, I was able to identify who I wanted in key positions and over the three years or so, began to orchestrate their development so they would be ready to step up when I entered the role."

3. Prioritization Takes on a Whole New Meaning

We heard story after story about the unrelenting 24/7 nature of the job and the importance of making lifestyle and priority changes to accommodate the unending demands of the role. Most CEOs spoke of the importance of exercising, eating right, and engaging in the most important outside activities. All spoke of the need to simplify their personal lives and to be highly selective about outside commitments. Most spoke about the importance of their "home identity" and remaining grounded within their CEO personae. While all reported feeling honored to have this important job, they also noted it required personal adjustments in order to do it well.

"I had no idea how physically demanding the job would be. For this job, I need to be energetic..."

Several CEOs talked about the importance of participating in select, family-based activities, such as coaching a child's sports team or being involved with their church/temple, and how critical it was for them to take vacations and weekends without taking calls at home. We heard a number of stories about the challenges of having so many different constituencies competing for their time with conflicting demands/requests and the importance of spending time on what truly matters most. All of the CEOs quickly discovered the importance of prioritization and time management—especially when so many good ideas/opportunities existed.

"I was surprised by the time management and prioritization challenges—both on internal and external things. I had to learn to say 'no' and to manage my time better."

"I was surprised as to the extent of external obligations for the CEO. I had a lot of learnings around prioritization, necessity of time requirements, and obligations that simply came with the job."

"I had no idea how physically demanding the job would be. For this job, I need to be energetic, focused, and disciplined all of the time."

"I don't think I had any real surprises when I became CEO. If there were any, it had to do with the intensity and significance of some issues versus the reality of the issues themselves."

"I was surprised by the unrelenting demands on my time from different constituencies. Demands come from employees, the communities in which we operate, investors, and especially Board members."

"My biggest surprise is that being CEO is as fun as it is."

"You have to have a lot of energy and be disciplined in how you use your time. I find time to do other things of importance to me—but it isn't by accident. It takes planning."

"I am inundated with data and information; it is simply not possible to digest it all. I have had to learn to discipline myself and decide what is really important, and concentrate on those items and schedule my time accordingly."

"I knew that the job of CEO would be demanding, but I was surprised at how much it truly infringes on my personal life. This is truly a 24/7 job. I find I must work evenings and weekends, and it can almost be overwhelming."

"The combination of regulatory and litigation issues demands an inordinate amount of time and attention. I was amazed at how much time these activities—such non–value-adding activities— diverted me from running the company."

4. Developing a Trusting Relationship with Your Board Is Essential

Every CEO spoke at length about the importance of his/her relationship with the Board. Some felt they had entered comfortable territory when they were named CEO because they had served on the Board for a number of years before becoming CEO. Most, however, did not sit on their company's Board of Directors prior to being named CEO. Some had the good fortune to sit on other Boards, which they described as being a highly worthwhile experience. However, many still commented that they wish they had been better prepared for the complex dynamics the collective and individual Board relationships presented to them.

> *"When I started, I told the Board I never want my compensation talked about or even to be a topic of conversation. I don't want any employee of this company to experience the humiliation of having to read about their CEO's compensation in the paper."*

In this era of corporate leadership, Board accountability has been heightened, and, of course, the liability that Board members now assume in their role underscores the scrutiny, challenge, and the rigor with which most Board members are discharging their duties. Concurrently, these factors of heightened visibility and liability make the investment of time, relationship management, dialogue, and education that CEOs are dedicating to their Board more significant than at any time in history. There are specific issues of working with difficult Board members and managing Board dynamics. Many CEOs wished they had acquired more experience with publicly traded Boards so they could have avoided some early pitfalls and missteps.

> *"I had a contentious relationship with the Board. For four years I didn't make much progress. It was a very tense environment with the Board and with the senior leaders. I had a hard time getting people to be courageous."*

"Our company had strong Board members when I became Chairman/CEO. My predecessor was very old school and didn't enjoy his interaction with the Board. His presentations to the Board were very scripted. He told them exactly what they had to know and nothing more. When I reflect back on starting this role, I would say that I was nowhere near adequately prepared to work with the Board. Through trial and error, I have become more proficient working with the Board, but it has not been easy for them or for me. I had not served on any outside Boards and now realize that it would have been an immensely helpful preparation for me."

"I probably felt the least prepared to deal with both a changing Board and changing strategy at the same time."

"I probably felt the least prepared to deal with both a changing Board and changing strategy at the same time."

"I spent a significant amount of time with the Board discussing the company's future and their vision for the company, but it wasn't clear that they held a common view. They did not seem to be as engaged in the company as other Boards I had worked with."

"I wish I would have had exposure to tools and ideas on establishing and managing relationships with different personalities of BOD members."

"I wish I had more Board experience and had participated in outside Boards. I had to learn to work with our Board through trial and error."

"I had been an active and voting member of the Board for three years prior to becoming CEO. My predecessor had me presenting and discussing the state of the company during that time. As a result, I got to know the Board members and they got to know me. Governance is not a difficult part of the job."

"I was not clear about the Board's responsibilities versus management's at first, and I found this a bit confusing. I was quickly mentored on this—but I was not clear about this from the outset of my tenure as CEO."

"I wish I would have had exposure to tools and ideas on establishing and managing relationships with different personalities of BOD members."

"Working with my Board is a non-issue. It was the company's Board when I took over as CEO. I think the key is communication. I communicate much more than my predecessor, and the Board loves it. I view them as my kitchen cabinet. On my Board, I have great friendships and advisors. In addition, I don't care if I am in this job, so I want to fight for the company, and the Board will either support my decisions and actions or not. I am prepared at all times for either. When I started, I told the Board I never want my compensation talked about or even to be a topic of conversation. I don't want any employee of this company to experience the humiliation of having to read about their CEO's compensation in the paper."

5. Transitioning Well Matters

An effective transition to the role of CEO is enormously important. Many of those interviewed shared their experiences and actions in making this transition, and what they wish they had known before they began. Clearly, the relationship of the new CEO with his/her predecessor is key, especially if the previous CEO will remain on the Board of Directors or will have any continuing role with the company. There were many stories about the benefits (or not) realized from working, consulting, or overlapping with a predecessor. In hindsight, all would have liked to benefit from the learnings of their predecessor, particularly in regard to people, customers, Board relations, and investments that were or were not made in the business.

"Succession is all about the successor: Picking the right person, making sure you don't overstay your term of effectiveness as sitting CEO."

Several talked about the importance of the first 100 days and how they should be used. Learnings from the CEOs who believed they made good use of those 100 days—and from the CEOs who felt they did not capitalize on that window—were shared openly and thoughtfully. It is important to acknowledge the successes of your predecessor and to show grace in recognizing his/her history with the company.

Common reflections included that the new CEO's values and vision should be explicitly communicated through his/her initial actions, decisions, and behaviors, and how he/she selects, manages, and leads the senior team and the organization, starting from day one. This, coupled with the comments about "scrutiny of every word and action," underscores the importance of transitioning well into this role, having a 100-day plan mapped out before entering the role, and moving quickly on leadership team composition. Listening well and traveling to the home cities of direct reports and Board members were all positive examples provided by those who realized the importance of this 100-day window of opportunity.

"Working hand-in-glove with the Chairman taught me much about his role, while he taught me much more about mine. If I was going to be a great CEO, I really had the highest probability of being successful given the training and exposure I had at this company."

"Once my successor is known, I will manage the transition period for the new CEO. The time of overlap between me and the incoming CEO should be relatively short—three to four months. It will need to be clear to everyone who is in charge; a longer overlap can become confusing to the organization and hamper the new CEO in regard to implementing changes."

"Succession is all about the successor: Picking the right person, making sure you don't overstay your term of effectiveness as sitting CEO. My predecessor was here many, many years. The first half of his tenure was better than his last half. When you hang on for too long, you start managing momentum versus real business performance or making important, future-focused decisions."

"Even though our company philosophy is to promote from within, there can still be issues when a final decision is made. I made it a point to be more open than my predecessor with my colleagues who were not chosen for the CEO role. I met with the two peers who were not selected the night I was named into the position. A week later we went to dinner. I knew I had a strong group of colleagues, and including them was important to me, but I also wanted to change the dynamics of our team. In this role you must be able to get the best out of all of the people within the organization. We spent time off-site to help build the new direction. All of us went through our delicacies—but in the end, we worked well together because we committed to do so and because it was the best thing for the company."

"In retrospect, I would have liked to have had one day a week with the previous CEO to talk about 'stuff that mattered.' I would have appreciated some early feedback and counsel from him on how to work with the Board, how to repair rifts among Board members, and how to create alignment among individuals with multiple agendas and objectives."

"I overlapped with my predecessor by about one year. I became CEO and he became Chairman. This worked out well, and I would recommend it for others. When he was CEO, he tended to control everything, but when he became Chairman, he did an about-face and did not meddle with management of the company. Rather, he helped me deal with Board issues and Board relationships. He understood the Board members and counseled me on managing these relationships. He did not tell me what to do or how to do it, but was a sounding board. If he had tried to tell me what to do or how to do it, the relationship would not have worked."

"I was the CFO for a period of time. I was able to understand all aspects of our finances and interact with the analysts who covered our company as part of investor relations. I had also led our marketing and manufacturing divisions. Additionally, I served as a group executive, which enabled me to work directly with the Chairman and with many divisions reporting to me."

"I quickly learned that the vehicles I had used for communicating as COO (such as formal slide decks) were no longer effective. Rather, I learned quickly that it was important for me to visit our various locations and to talk with people about their businesses. In some ways, I found this refreshing because these conversations brought me back to the reasons the company exists. I have also learned to communicate more clearly and succinctly. This was a particularly challenging task because of the geographic diversity, the size of our employee population, and the fact that fewer than half of our employees speak English."

"I wasn't told this, but I believe I was identified as one of a number of candidates to become CEO almost 15 years ago. A few of us entered a series of career rotations that, in retrospect, were designed to give us relevant experiences and also to begin to assess our fit. As a company, we have been very disciplined on how we have gone about succession planning."

6. Unending Governance Challenges

Another area mentioned by nearly all of the CEO interviewees was how significantly things have changed in the past seven or so years with respect to investor relations, government relations, regulatory bodies, and the need to feed a constantly streaming news media. CEOs spoke about how they had received formal training in investor/government relations, media, etc., but that they are now leading in an era where the demands are far greater and more complicated than they were when they first got started. We heard stories that, in the course of their tenures as CEOs, the external environment had changed from "play by the rules" and "do the right thing and everything will be fine" to one where external sources relentlessly try to prove that you have done

> *". . . significant changes in corporate governance had begun to occur in American industry..."*

something wrong or are somehow not in compliance, even when the company had done nothing wrong and, in fact, was in compliance. Nearly all the CEOs listed this area among the top two or three things that they wished they were better prepared to handle prior to becoming CEO.

"At just about the time I became CEO, significant changes in corporate governance had begun to occur in American industry. These changes mandated that we make significant changes in our governance. Architecting and leading these changes and ensuring compliance have taken a great deal of my time and of the Board's time. We strengthened our governance processes and the capabilities of the people involved. The result has been beneficial, but it has required a lot of work, including restructuring and finding new talent. It has also been a distraction for the Board at times."

"I was not well-prepared for the political/media/government relations/investor relations part of the job. I had formal training in each of those areas, but the requirements of these things are so different from when I first became CEO. There are huge IR challenges and pressures coming at us from the external environment that continue to intensify."

"In addition to having to 'right the ship' when I became CEO, the Board and I had to face dramatic changes in the regulatory environment, such as Sarbanes-Oxley. This meant we had to address issues of governance, including the role of the Board and the inherent liabilities that were now made explicit."

"The year of the Sarbanes-Oxley Act (SOX) implementation took a lot out of the organization. The manual work required was immense. I was not prepared for this."

"One significant challenge has been working with various regulatory agencies and the orientation of their members. In some ways, I had a naïve view that if we communicated with the agencies and told them what we were doing, and if I answered their questions candidly, we would move forward together. What I discovered is that they are adversarial by nature. They operate with a mind-set that seeks to find something to accuse you of. It took me a while to realize this and know how to handle this."

"One thing that surprised me was the extent to which it appears that the regulatory environment is out of control. Regulatory agencies often appear to have only secondary interest in assuring compliance and in helping companies meet the regulatory requirements. Rather, they appear to be more interested in scrutinizing every possible thing a company does in order to find problems and thereby demonstrate to the public that they are doing their jobs. This serves to further their own agendas while punishing the companies and diverting valuable company resources from truly value-adding activities. I had assumed that these agencies would be more interested in helping us with compliance and enabling us to be more competitive globally but that does not appear to be the case. Rather, adversarial relationships seem to be what they favor."

7. Public Scrutiny: No Private Life

Almost everyone interviewed stated that he/she knew that life would change when they became CEO. They knew they would be "busy," and they knew that people would be watching what they did. What surprised many was the magnitude and intensity of the scrutiny they would be subjected to. Suddenly they realized that not only was the job 24/7, but it was one that required them to be visible and "on" at almost all times. Along with this scrutiny comes public commentary and often criticism. The CEO becomes the tangible representation of the enterprise. This visibility and scrutiny extends to their family as well. Finally, along with the visibility and scrutiny, people watch and listen carefully to a CEO's actions and words, whose meanings often become magnified.

> *"I did not realize how public my life as CEO would be..."*

"I wish I had more personal coaching about being a CEO. You are 'on' all of the time. You are influencing and being influenced with every conversation."

"Everyone reads into everything. You are being watched all of the time. The media writes about you endlessly."

"I did not realize how public my life as CEO would be. It was much more than I ever imagined. From my compensation to the business news coverage—it is unrelenting."

"I was surprised by the impact of what I say or do. I found that I have to be careful when I talk because others are likely to magnify my comments or assume that as I think out loud, I am giving them directions. People often take me much more seriously than I intend."

"I was not prepared for the examination of every word out of my mouth. If I ask for a glass of water, people give me a reservoir."

"I did not know how the demands of being CEO would be so different from those of running an operation. I didn't realize the public scrutiny or how people would criticize me and my family. It takes a toll professionally and personally."

"I was not prepared for the instant stardom. I moved to a larger city, in part, for the anonymity."

"As CEO, I am subject to an amazing level of scrutiny, and with the scrutiny, enormous criticism. This occurs in the press, in shareholder meetings, and in journals and magazines. Although the criticism may be tough on me, it can be especially difficult for my family."

"I knew that because of the nature of our business and the role of the CEO, I would be highly visible. I knew that I had to go 'on stage' almost all of the time, but this visibility also extends to the family in both positive and negative ways."

"The CEO title has greater impact in some ways on the spouse and family than it does on the incumbent. My wife and kids read about me in the press, some of it flattering and some not, and some of it is factual and some of it is simply not true. They even write about my wife."

"It is important to be a realistic optimist. I can't walk into an elevator with a frown on my face or people will think there's a problem. As the leader of the company I have to be a cheerleader and encourager about things, while being realistic about the situation. The fact is, you are being watched all of the time, and people will draw their own conclusions based on facial gestures and more subtle things. I also have to be willing to accept feedback when my behavior has led to unintended interpretations."

8. Isolation of the Job

One observation from almost 100% of the participating CEOs was how isolated they feel in the job. They spoke with great clarity about how their relationships with others changed on day one of their being named CEO. Longstanding relationships and friendships changed overnight. Few people shared information with them anymore, and what was shared was often filtered. They also spoke of the need to compensate for their isolation and have friends or colleagues with whom they could discuss the many things that they might contemplate, wonder about, or want to consider for the future of the company.

"The minute I was announced as the new CEO, every relationship changed. Everyone wanted to know what I thought or wanted before they would say anything."

"Everyone is looking for something from you. I did not expect the CEO title to color everyone's point of view of who I was."

"I have to continually work at keeping lines of communication open with the rest of the organization. No one really wants to drop in and have an informal conversation, and no one wants to tell me things they think I don't want to hear."

"One thing that surprised me was how alone I felt once I was in the role of CEO. I could understand this sense of being alone if I had been an outside hire, but I had been with the company for over 20 years. In this role, I really have no peers. I really do not think that I changed personally, but by the very nature of the role, I no longer had any peers to talk with on an informal basis. As a result, many things can be happening in the company that I don't hear about —things that I would like to know. To address this, I established a 'kitchen cabinet' of just a few people, and we meet three or four times a year to talk about what is happening in the company. The members of this kitchen cabinet provide me with an outside and unbiased perspective of events and of how I am doing. The kitchen cabinet has been an important source of information for me."

"One thing that has struck me is how alone this role can make me feel. I am really on my own. There might be one or two people with whom I can have a candid conversation, but even those are, by necessity, limited in scope."

"As soon as I was named CEO, my relationships changed—even longstanding ones—overnight. Also, the nature of information others brought to me changed and the amount of information shrank."

"I was surprised by how isolating the role is. You get very little information flow, and it can get very isolated. You can sit in your office and think everything is fine and never know that it is not [fine]. You have to force yourself to go out and talk with people."

"Once I became CEO, it was as if I became a different person overnight. It was as if I became a celebrity and whatever I did or said was taken more seriously than before. Furthermore, I no longer get the same level of information about what is going on inside the company like I once did; people are less candid with me. This is true even of some of my older and longstanding relationships. I simply stopped getting the same candor as before. Everyone became instantly less inclined to give me information. I have had to find ways to reach out and get what I consider really useful information. The normal channels do not provide it. I have had to find the few people who will be candid with me. People just seem to be more remote, and they distance themselves from me."

"I would say that one thing that a person cannot be prepared for is the emotional aspect of knowing that you are the final step in a decision-making process that can affect tens of billions of dollars and thousands of employees. The CEO has ultimate accountability, and this can be a lonely feeling sometimes."

Summary

In summary, the CEOs in this study spoke with great sincerity, candor, and humility as they shared their experiences and learnings, and described "what-I-wish-I-had-knowns" with Braksick and Hillgren. Their stories, told with great emotion and conviction, further emphasized the significance of these challenges.

We were struck at the overt absence of the "what-I-wish-I-had-knowns" that conventional wisdom might lead us to think would be great challenges to these men and women, such as working in third-world countries, integrating huge acquisitions, deciding which business units to nurture and which to divest, coping with commodity costs as they increase 300+% above budgeted/forecast levels in a down economy, shifting assets to adjust to increasing amounts of business stemming from outside the U.S., and so on. However, these were not the areas they felt ill-prepared to handle. That observation should not be lost on the reader. The CEOs felt extremely well-prepared for these challenges—those that make up the core business accountabilities.

What they felt the least prepared for were the personal and interpersonal elements of the role—the unrelenting public scrutiny and challenges imposed by governance systems, processes, and people. Then there were feelings of isolation in being a leader atop a major global corporation, who looks right and left, up and down, and sees no one inside the company, sitting alongside, racing to his/her office to share information they might not like to hear—but desperately want to know. They recognized the need to make certain they were doing everything in their power to reinforce the behavior of telling them bad news—and engage their team members in collaborative and objective problem solving.

They felt unprepared for the absence of someone with whom they could talk, problem solve, and think outside the box, who had no vested interest or consequences attached. For those conversations, they engineered special groups or went outside their companies, quite often turning to an executive coach, predecessor, or their spouse, finding the much-needed place where they could simply be their normal, imperfect selves.

The CEO
PART II Prerequisites

AUTHOR
James S. Hillgren, Ph.D.
The Continuous Learning Group, Inc. (CLG)

CONTRIBUTING WRITER
Jennifer Howard
The Continuous Learning Group, Inc. (CLG)

In the course of the interviews with the sitting CEOs, the participants described factors they believed were particularly significant in their preparation for fulfilling the role. The first set of factors included personal qualities and attributes, as well as innate abilities, which they developed very early in life (Chapter 4).

The second set of factors included the unique career opportunities and experiences that helped them develop the specific competencies that would later prove integral in leading their enterprise (Chapter 5).

The third and final set of factors included management practices adopted during the course of their careers that they found particularly helpful in preparing and in entering the role of CEO (Chapter 6).

Part II of this report summarizes and details the attributes, experiences, and managerial practices shared by these CEOs in our interviews with them.

FOUR

Personal Qualities and Attributes

The personal attributes that emerged from the interviews included six qualities that the CEOs felt were instrumental to their success. These included:

1. Integrity — Candor, follow-through, and delivery on commitments; taking actions that are consistent with stated values even if inconsistent with prior organizational practices.

2. Courage — The personal willingness to be decisive and adhere to an unpopular decision, to remove people who are former peers from their roles in the organization, or to take the company in a direction others feel is risky.

3. Intellectual Curiosity and Continuous Learning — Viewing events (including failures) as learning opportunities and maintaining a constant curiosity about people, the outside world, and other industries; having a routine of reading, attending selected conferences, and taking advantage of ongoing educational opportunities.

4. Resilience — The ability to cope with constant questioning, criticism, and scrutiny by various constituencies such as shareholders, Board members, the press, analysts, government regulators, employees, and political groups.

5. Self-awareness and Humility — The practice of frequent self-assessment and actively identifying personal shortcomings to understand, address, or compensate for them; to have natural regard and admiration for the talents that others bring to the organization to create a space for others to express themselves.

6. Dispassionate Compassion — The ability to remove oneself from allowing one's past and personal relationships to color decision making about the business, while still holding strong empathy for those constituencies that the CEO serves.

1. Integrity

The interviews reflected how important integrity is to this role and how each CEO made symbolic gestures in his/her own way to demonstrate that they intended to live up to the values that they aspired to in their positions. This could take the form of being very deliberate in their communications to the organization or demonstrating how they reached out to the members of their senior team (and their families). Many interviewees mentioned that they had underestimated the impact of everything they did or said, making them realize that behaving very consistently with their stated values at all times was an unstated requirement of the job.

> *"Together, the CEO and the COO have to own and be in the forefront of exhibiting the values of the company, and they must commit the resources to develop those same behaviors in others."*

> *"I didn't realize how hurt this company was by things in its past and how betrayed people felt."*

> *"I had to do so much around communications."*

> *"I send correspondence to parents and spouses of my executive team. This is very important to me."*

> *"I know that it is important to attend to peoples' hearts and heads. I, and the senior team, must work from an inverted organizational pyramid. The position of the senior leadership team is at the bottom of the pyramid, and our role is to enable others to perform and to remove obstacles for them."*

> *"Together, the CEO and the COO have to own and be in the forefront of exhibiting the values of the company, and they must commit the resources to develop those same behaviors in others."*

> *"The great corporate myth is that what happens in the executive office is 'secret,' but in truth, employees and even external audiences 'worth their salt' are able to figure out what is occurring. It is better to be transparent and honest with this information than to continue to kid ourselves and believe it is hidden."*

2. COURAGE

Stories and anecdotes reflected the courage it takes to be in the top slot of an organization. It took on many forms, from exiting former peers and, in some cases, former bosses who weren't competent, to being decisive and changing the strategy of the company. In some cases it meant "undoing" the work of their predecessor or having to say "no" to a lot of good ideas. The CEO role is clearly not for the faint of heart. One needs a strong inner core to be able to succeed in this position.

"I realize that the decisions I make now as CEO are gray and non-reversible, yet I have to make people believe that it's the right thing to do. Even if a decision is 51 to 49, I need to sell them that it is a 'go.'"

"Those team members who wouldn't engage, I let them go. I needed people to shout and argue with me."

"When I was assigned my first international leadership role, I realized all the top positions were held by U.S. expatriates. The local nationals in each country were very concerned that there was not any representation by the local management in consideration of their culture and their ways of life. Getting the leadership team right, from multiple perspectives, meant that less senior people were put into more positions of authority. However it turned out to be 100% the right thing to do."

"When I became CEO, times were good and there was a temptation to add headcount as well as expand other resources. Everything folks were bringing forward sounded like a good idea. I just had to say 'no.'"

"Intuition and courage are key to this position. Use both to develop your priorities to make things happen."

"As I look ahead, profit and continued growth require bold moves."

"Companies in our space were consolidating. Therefore, we needed to consolidate our brands. This required radical changes in our strategy and in our culture that were tough on the organization."

"My boss thought my strategy was wrong. The conversation I dreaded for a year only took six minutes to have . . . about changing the business model. My boss even helped me work the changes through the Board."

"There is a challenge on how to set a bold agenda for the company and drive it to make it happen. I believe that this knowledge comes from a combination of experiential learning, bold moves, bold decisions, framing, and sticking to it. Oftentimes there is only 50% buy-in at the time a decision gets made. It is at this point that I must have the courage of conviction to still go with that decision and bring along the other 50%. I know the buck stops with me. Courage comes from watching others trying, and pulling them up when they fail. So, in this role, if you think something needs to be done, then change it. Anything that is not working well or right in the company is my responsibility. I can point no fingers."

". . . Anything that is not working well or right in the company is my responsibility. I can point no fingers."

3. Intellectual Curiosity and Continuous Learning

The importance of not becoming complacent and ensuring that he/she remained current on events and the state of the business came out loud and clear in the interviews. One commonly mentioned challenge is that few people inside companies seem to be comfortable having candid or spontaneous conversations with their CEOs. It appears that the days of "throwing around ideas for intellectual debate" are insufficient relative to the CEO's need for such stimulating conversations. The CEOs interviewed as part of this study are responding to that gap by creating their own vehicles for intellectual debate and continuous learning.

" . . . we recognize that we have to get involved and respond at a global level to these challenges and pressures. We can't NOT get involved."

"Get an executive coach to help you make the transition... to discuss problems with and to problem-solve around things such as the interpersonal challenges of managing former peers."

"I think it is helpful to remain connected to the rest of the world... it is so easy to just get caught up in your CEO role and responsibilities. At both the personal and professional level, it is important to maintain a working knowledge of what is happening in society."

"As a global company, we have to recognize how much of the world dynamics have changed. As part of the external environment, we recognize that there are huge investor relationship challenges and pressures that continue to intensify. We recognize that we have to get involved and respond at a global level to these challenges and pressures. We can't NOT get involved."

"I spend a lot of time going to conferences, looking and learning outside of the organization. Specifically, I look for things that we are not seeing in the organization and looking for the most challenging point of view."

"I continuously learn to keep my curiosity on fire."

"Participation in the American Society of Corporate Executives has been extremely useful. It is a roundtable of approximately 30 CEOs, each of whom is invited to the membership and who represents a unique business segment or industry."

"I do a lot of reading on leadership and talent planning. I think this is a key role for the CEO, and I would advise my successor to continually keep abreast of current thinking on leadership and talent management."

"Participation in the American Society of Corporate Executives has been extremely useful. It is a roundtable of approximately 30 CEOs, each of whom is invited to the membership and who represents a unique business segment or industry."

4. RESILIENCE

Much was shared in the CEO interviews regarding how taxing this role was— mentally, physically, and emotionally. The interviewees shared the difficulty of always feeling "on" no matter how few people were around. Stories were shared about choosing to live in big cities or small towns just to have some anonymity and freedom from every word and gesture being scrutinized by others. Spouses and children also were affected, either by absence of the parent, traveling as the spouse of the CEO, or even being criticized at school for a parent's decision. Staying healthy, eating and sleeping well, and keeping outside social functions to a minimum became very important for success in this role.

"I don't drink. I stay in shape. I have one job, one wife. I lead a simple life. I had no idea how physically demanding this job would be. To be successful, I need to be energetic, focused, and disciplined."

"My family has a way of keeping me centered. When I go home, I am not the CEO—I am the person who takes out the garbage. My family is very important to me, and understanding the importance of balance in my life helps me understand how important it is to help others manage their work-life balance as well."

"I would advise my successor to be prepared to address three important things:
1. There will be enormous demands on your time, and you must set priorities for your time
2. You must work to keep lines of communication open
3. You will be inundated with information, and you must derive a method to identify what is important."

"I don't have much of a social life. I just like to spend time with my family where I don't have to feel 'on.'"

"As CEO, I am subject to an amazing level of scrutiny, and with the scrutiny, enormous criticism. This occurs in the press, in shareholder meetings, and in journals and magazines. Although the criticism can be tough on me, it can be especially difficult for my family."

"I don't drink. I stay in shape. I have one job, one wife. I lead a simple life. I had no idea how physically demanding this job would be. To be successful, I need to be energetic, focused, and disciplined."

"I didn't realize how public my life as the CEO would be; it was much more than I imagined... from my compensation to the business news coverage."

"The role of the CEO is very taxing and requires long hours and extensive travel. This takes time away from my family and personal life. The support from my strong family has been key. You must be aligned in your values in order to do this work."

"I knew that because of the nature of our business and the role of the CEO, I would be highly visible. I knew I had to be 'on stage' almost all of the time, but this visibility also extends to the family in both positive and negative ways. For example, when I first became CEO, I was about to address a large group of employees. Just before I took the podium, I learned that my son, who at that time worked for the company, had been assaulted. Apparently this occurred because he had been identified as my son—the son of the CEO."

5. Self-Awareness and Humility

The CEOs each shared stories of lessons learned from their past that taught them the importance of recognizing their own shortcomings and how they had learned to set priorities and surround themselves with competent people they could rely on. They also realized that while they needed to convey confidence, boldness, and decisiveness, the world is a complex system and disaster could be around the next corner.

"Just as I work at understanding others, I have to make sure I know myself. I have to know my weaknesses and blind spots and either correct them or find a way to compensate..."

"Never forget that in this job, you are only as good as you did last quarter."

"When I became CEO, the company's performance had been good for the past five consecutive years. The company had strong earnings growth. While there was an increase in the confidence in the environment, I personally didn't feel as confident because the horizon didn't look good. Today we live in an ecosystem with so many variables and things happening. I find that winning today gives you no certainty of winning tomorrow."

"I believe that there is a lot I don't know, so I am a permanent student."

"The challenge is to leave your ego at the door. You have to have some, but we need to step back and keep the rest of the system running."

"The new CEO must be willing to look at data objectively and be willing to admit mistakes in the face of the data."

"My time in the military was invaluable. I learned early that in pursuing a mission, people come first. Without people being totally committed, we could not achieve our mission. This means that I had to earn the respect and trust of the people in my command and that they knew that I had their best interests at heart. This is important not only for me, but for leadership at all levels. That is why I think it is important to evaluate and coach my direct reports in regard to their interpersonal skills and that they do the same with their direct reports."

"There is a high failure rate of CEOs."

"Self-awareness is an important attribute in dealing with the stress inherent in the role. In fact, self-evaluation needs to be an ongoing activity."

"Just as I work at understanding others, I have to make sure I know myself. I have to know my weaknesses and blind spots and either correct them or find a way to compensate. I have to continually learn, and learning along with insight helps build resiliency."

"The CEO must understand what he/she is good at and then make sure the people around him/her are good at what the CEO is not good at. This means the CEO must be self-aware and avail himself/ herself of someone to challenge their thinking and self-assessment."

"I believe one of the most important things I can do is to understand my own strengths and weaknesses. I have to do this in an objective and introspective manner, and I have to engage in some form of reality testing regarding my self-assessment. By knowing my strengths, weaknesses, and blind spots, I can begin to develop compensatory mechanisms. Without this knowledge, I cannot adequately compensate and, hence, cannot adequately lead."

6. Dispassionate Compassion

While these terms might seem contradictory, it is evident that successful CEOs need to make objective and dispassionate decisions about the talent on their team and in their organization, often making difficult decisions about people with whom they have had a long-standing relationship. At the same time, compassion and empathy are critical to understanding and addressing the needs of the various constituents that the CEO serves—the shareholders, the employees, and the BOD—and to developing a loyal and engaged organization.

"I learned early that I must act dispassionately and objectively with my relationships with people and make decisions about people and business units that potentially conflicted with old loyalties. As CEO, my responsibilities, decisions, and actions deal with intangible issues and their impact, and outcomes are not always readily apparent."

"One of my regrets is not acting on personnel issues more quickly. I found myself facing problematic performance and inappropriate behavior in some staff, and I believe I allowed it to continue longer than I should have."

"I gave everyone on the team six months to prove himself. I was wonderful to everyone and worked closely to help and support them. No one left my team feeling badly."

"Becoming the CEO required me to become a different person. I had to develop and adopt behaviors that were different than the behaviors that got me to this role. I found that I had to act with dispassionate objectivity, separating myself from personal and professional loyalties. This meant moving people and disposing of business units."

"I am very people-oriented despite the fact that I changed out most of our leadership team. My core values are: Believe in people; delegate; hold people accountable; be fact-based and objective; integrity above all else."

"I had a few people who just did not get this; they did not accept how we were going to change. In a couple of cases this was really disappointing because they were talented people and were friends. I had to let them go."

SUMMARY

All of the CEOs interviewed had strong opinions about the attributes one must possess to be a successful CEO. While the specific stories of how these attributes were tested varied across the CEOs we spoke with, the importance of courage, integrity, intellectual curiosity/being a continuous learner, resilience, selfawareness/humility, and dispassionate compassion in the success of these individuals, was remarkably consistent. It is clear that the role and challenges of being CEO test the very core of an individual and rely on strength and wisdom that comes from within.

FIVE

CAREER EXPERIENCES

A second important set of ingredients required to prepare for the CEO role, as described by the participants in this study, included the skills, competencies, and lessons learned from prior career experiences. Nine specific past experiences repeatedly were cited as those that were pivotal to the readiness and confidence of the CEO in his/her new role. This section provides an invaluable set of data for those charged with strategic talent management and development of future CEO candidates, and for those aspiring to one day be the CEO of a major global corporation. These experiences included:

1. **Living and Working Outside the United States**
2. **Running a Standalone P&L**
3. **Having Strong Foundational Competence, Especially Strategy**
4. **Leading Frontline Operations**
5. **Having Experience in All Aspects of the Business**
6. **Working with Different Constituencies**
7. **Sitting on Other Boards**
8. **Learning Through People**
9. **Learning Through Crises**

1. LIVING AND WORKING OUTSIDE THE U.S.

Repeatedly, we heard the importance of global exposure, and it was emphasized that one needed to live there, not just visit. The benefits came in two primary forms:

- The first is an assignment in one or more parts of the world to provide the CEO candidate with an awareness and appreciation of other cultures and of the value that such diversity brings. It tends to cause one to surrender any vestiges of ethnocentrism.

- The second is providing leadership in one or more different cultures in order to understand the commonalities and differences in effective leadership styles in diverse cultures. This enables the leader to see the world through the eyes of others and truly appreciate the global nature of the industry and the company.

"I have lived and worked in a global environment since I was 19 years old. As a result, I have enormous respect for differences and how they shape how work gets done."

"I spent four years in Asia and four years in Europe running businesses there. That was absolutely key to my understanding of what it meant to run a global company."

"International experience is also critical in developing a much broader perspective in how other cultures work and think..."

"A lot of companies look at individuals for whom English is not their first language as being knowledgeable if they can speak in understandable English. People who have run businesses outside the U.S. know that's not necessarily the case. It's not always necessary to speak English in order to be an extremely astute business person."

"Living and working internationally is key. I had to learn different cultures, different cost structures, different ways of working. I spent five years in Europe and three years in Indonesia."

"I lived in Kazakhstan, Venezuela, and Vancouver. This is critical experience to successfully run a global company."

"International experience is also critical in developing a much broader perspective in how other cultures work and think. This has helped me understand different markets and what is motivational to people in other cultures."

"One thing I had not had in my background, but I knew that I needed, was international experience. I needed to understand the complexities of different geographic, political, and cultural environments. I immersed myself in international issues for about six months to try to get up to speed."

I have lived and worked in a global environment since I was 19 years old. As a result, I have enormous respect for differences and how they shape how work gets done."

"Having three children and working at four assignments in four countries, all in the first five and a half years of my career with this company, was an immersion in valuable experience

2. Running a Standalone P&L

Many CEOs indicated that having responsibility for managing a major integrated organizational unit with P&L responsibility served them well in their preparation for this role. It was particularly important to be in place long enough to see and own the impact of the decisions they made while in that role, and to see how those decisions affected the unit's short- and long-term results.

"My best preparation was running a real P&L with no costs from above, nothing fake."

"My best preparation was running a real P&L with no costs from above, nothing fake."

"I learned that no strategy trumps excellence in execution."

"I had great experience in the company prior to becoming CEO of the enterprise. I had many opportunities to try and fail, to see what works, and to learn from my mistakes. I ran a standalone P&L outside of the U.S., and that provided a great venue for me to learn so much. The coaching/mentoring I received from the previous CEO was helpful."

"At 32 years of age I was running a $100-million to $150-million business unit in my first company."

3. Having Strong Foundational Competence, Especially Strategy

Being strong in some area of organizational competence, whether it's finance, operations, marketing, or sales, was cited as providing a CEO with a platform to contribute deep understanding of various business levers, as well as meaning there were fewer things for one to learn as they took over the role.

"I believe that to be effective, the CEO must have some foundational skill, one that the CEO is particularly good at. Mine is marketing and brand management, but it could be finance or some other area."

"No matter how good an executive is in his/her prior industry, or even industries, they will not have the sharp and deep instincts obtainable only by significant time immersed in their current industry trying things, seeing results, and learning from those experiences."

"I had the valuable opportunity of being a CEO for a smaller company. It had research, branding, etc., all of its own. The whole experience was invaluable in building my confidence and competence to run a large, global company."

"The keys to my success were the career assignments I had and the mentoring I received along the way. I felt incredibly well prepared to move into the CEO role, and I attribute that largely to those two factors."

4. Leading Frontline Operations

A number of CEOs indicated that, at a minimum, rotation through a position that entails leading and directing frontline operations is important. This not only gives one true understanding and empathy for that role, but it also builds credibility in the eyes of the frontline employee.

"It is critical to remember that the most important people in the organization are the frontline employees—the people who create and deliver value to the customer."

"I believe that the CEO should have some exposure to managing the core operating functions of the business. This way the CEO will know what is truly important to the frontline employees as they perform their jobs. This will also develop credibility and trust between the CEO and the front line."

"As far as I am concerned, the only way to get into a corporate role (like CEO) is to have worked in the field."

"My career in this company benefited greatly from the opportunity to get some early 'work face' experience, and then some broader managerial—and ultimately executive—experience, prior to being named CEO."

"As far as I am concerned, the only way to get into a corporate role (like CEO) is to have worked in the field."

---

5. Having Experience in All Aspects of the Business

It is particularly helpful if the CEO has held leadership roles in all or most of the significant functions of the business. Recognizing the complexity of the "ecosystem" that makes up the breadth of the enterprise often falls uniquely to the CEO role. Every action causes another equal and powerful reaction. Recognizing this can make decisions quite complex.

"I was very fortunate in the positions that I have held in other organizations. These experiences have played a significant role in preparing me for my current position. I have been in major sales positions, marketing and operations. In these roles I have learned how to engage people at various levels in the company and how to communicate an organization's strategy in a straightforward and understandable fashion."

"I had done the IR side, and I knew the analysts that covered our space. I had run manufacturing and marketing. If I was going to be a great CEO, I really had the highest probability of being successful given the previous training and exposure I'd had."

"As a group executive, I worked directly with the Chairman and had many of the divisions reporting to me. Working hand-in-glove with our Chairman taught me much about his role and allowed him to teach me more about mine."

---

6. WORKING WITH DIFFERENT CONSTITUENCIES

Almost all of the CEOs indicated that either they had fairly extensive exposure and experience working with various constituencies, which served them well, or they had too limited exposure to these groups, which was a significant drawback to their early effectiveness. These constituency groups included market analysts, Boards of Directors, the press, government regulators, and community leaders.

"One thing I have learned is how important it is to maintain strong relationships with vendors, communities, and other diverse constituencies..."

"I began doing investment relations road shows four to five years before becoming CEO. This was a great risk by my CEO. This part of the transition went extremely well. My boss was right not to do this when it would be OK to make mistakes. The way you speak to the investment community is completely different from how you communicate with anyone else."

"The investor community was new to me. I had to learn quickly how to talk to investors and analysts. I was a bit surprised by how much depth I had to go into with them."

"I had done the IR side of the business and knew the analysts that covered our space. I had run marketing, manufacturing. If I was going to be a great CEO, I really had the highest probability of being successful given the training and exposure I had gotten during my career."

"I am active on a number of Boards, including profit and non-profit organizations. I find these to be important to me to keep me fresh and to provide me with an ever broader perspective on what other organizations are doing, but it is also a way of returning value to the various communities in which we operate or where we have influence."

"One thing I have learned is how important it is to maintain strong relationships with vendors, communities, and other diverse constituencies. We dedicate a lot of time and money to maintaining strong ties with communities and community organizations and we try to work closely with our business partners. This is both part of our corporate responsibility and is also important from an image standpoint. I have served as the CFO, so I know that I cannot point to the direct payback this might have, but I know that it is integral to the long-term strategy of the business."

"We are in a highly regulated industry..."

"In retrospect, one area that I have found that we did not handle as well as we could have is the transition of key commercial relationships. During my predecessor's tenure he built up strong personal and commercial relationships with a number of significant business partners. These people and their firms formed ties with us due in large part to the personal relationships that he established. I believe that these strong ties were 60% personal and 40% commercial."

"We are in a highly regulated industry and, therefore, relationships with regulators, federal administrators, the White House, legislators, governors, and others are very important. My predecessor was quite good at these and had very deep relationships. We did not transfer these as well as we could have. To make up for this, I am spending an inordinate amount of time developing these ties, getting to know people in these roles, and getting them to know me."

7. Sitting on Other Boards

A number of the CEOs indicated that they participated on Boards prior to becoming CEO, and even more are participating on Boards since becoming CEO. The findings indicate that this experience has been invaluable in providing the CEO with skills in working with his or her own Board members and in understanding the issues in confronting and driving the dynamics of Board management relations.

"One thing that has been helpful to me has been my participation on Boards of other companies. This participation requires a great deal of my time, but it is well worth it. I am able to see how other companies operate, thus giving me a different perspective. More importantly, I can see that other companies are facing challenges similar to ours, and we are not alone."

"I am on two outside Boards, which have been very helpful learning experiences for me."

"I have been on Boards of other companies for the past several years. This has enabled me to see how they operate. They are very different from us, but equally successful."

"Prior to becoming CEO, I had served on the Board for two years. This time with the Board was invaluable in providing insights on how our Board worked and the personalities of the various Board members, and it allowed me to become comfortable working with them."

"I was able to learn about Board leadership through my position as CEO of a standalone company within our company and by watching and learning through my senior staff position. I had good coaching from my predecessor, and I try now to share a lot with my direct reports so they, too, can learn about what happens when they are in the room with the Board and when they are not."

8. LEARNING THROUGH PEOPLE

Many of the CEOs talked about lessons they had learned through working with people and relationships that were important to them. Some of these came from being a leader to others, but many also came from being someone's protégé or from just learning to work on a team.

"I've been a soccer player for 40 years. On a soccer field, everyone is equal… no one is more special than the next person. I have found this to be a good lesson in managing people and running a business."

"Critical to my success and preparation for this role is the time I spend with people. I spend one-third of my working time with people. I worked hard at this as I was coming up through the company. This was a big plus for me coming into this role."

"I had excellent on-the-job training for each of my promotions and job changes. My bosses were my best mentors, and I was able to make mistakes and learn along the way."

"External coaches have been very helpful to me in my growth. Feedback is key in any regard."

"I had a fantastic boss for seven years in the U.K. who mentored and coached me to be a great leader."

"I have had a good deal of experience in assessing and developing leadership talent. I am still getting to know some of the talent in the organization, but I can fairly quickly judge an individual's strengths and weaknesses and determine how they might be developed. (This skill has served me well in this role.)"

"From my past roles, I have learned how to build trust and credibility through candor, honesty, and meeting commitments. When I do this, I believe that relationships will last a lifetime."

9. LEARNING THROUGH CRISES

In addition to learning through people, a number of the CEOs commented on how important it is to have learned through events, i.e., confronted situations that placed them well outside their comfort zones. In these circumstances, the CEOs commented that they learned to confront difficult events that had unknown outcomes. These experiences included dealing with crises and succeeding, but just as important, dealing with crises and failing. The CEOs commented that it is a crucial lesson to learn that people can fail but that they must maintain their confidence and continue if they are going to eventually succeed.

> *"The CEO must have a great deal of stamina and resolve."*

"One thing that helped me was my participation in sports. It taught me that I could fail and fail and fail, and that I could learn from these failures and come back to win."

"I went through crises in other companies before coming to this one and turned them around. I don't think you would want someone as a CEO who has not faced a crisis and won, and who has not faced a crisis and lost. People are tested by failure."

"I have been an officer in other companies and have seen some difficult times. I have faced these crises with my fellow officers, and in some we have succeeded, and in some we did not. I came into the role battle-hardened. As a result, I have learned not to despair, not to lose confidence, and not become fearful that we might not make it. You can't go into a crisis thinking you might fail."

"The CEO must have a great deal of stamina and resolve. The person must be able to take multiple 'blows' and setbacks, and still come back for more."

"I have landed on a crude approach to crisis management, as follows:
- *Above all, stay balanced and be alert to important feedback*
- *Stay laser-focused on the critical success factors within your control*
- *Play the cards you have while always watching for new, helpful cards*
- *Get traction, lean forward, hope for the best, plan for the worst."*

Summary

In summary, the experiences called out by these CEOs as those that best prepared them for the job were ones that took them outside their comfort zone, that stretched/challenged them significantly, and that, through the eyes of others, taught them more about their company, their customers, their employees, the regions in which their company does business, and themselves. Interestingly, even those CEOs who came from the outside reported identical paths to their preparation for becoming CEO, thus suggesting that it is the experiences themselves that are important, rather than the fact that those experiences occurred in the companies where they would later become CEO.

SIX

MANAGEMENT PRACTICES
I HAVE LEARNED

In addition to the personal attributes and prior work experiences that participating CEOs described as important to assuming their role, there was a high degree of consistency in the nature of the management practices that they have adopted and have learned to do consistently and well. These are practices and tools they have developed over time in various leadership roles. The CEOs believe it is these practices that make a significant contribution to establishing a consistent course for the enterprise, to engendering passion in others for that course, and in enhancing the enterprise's leadership bench strength. The practices shared by these CEOs are summarized in the following nine areas:

1. **Engage and Motivate Others Without Relying on Financial Rewards or Threats**

2. **Let Go of Things I Used to Do Well**

3. **Be Clear About the Behaviors and Competencies I Want to See in Others—and Serve as a Role Model**

4. **Be Clear and Relentless About Our Direction**

5. **Provide Others with Timely Feedback and Acknowledgement**

6. **Encourage Divergent Opinions**

7. **Assess and Act on Competency and Performance Issues**

8. **Use Candor in Communications**

9. **Collaborate**

1. Engage and Motivate Others Without Relying on Financial Rewards or Threats

A number of the CEOs in the study indicated that early in their careers they learned how important it is to engage the hearts and minds of others, and to do so without relying on tangible and monetary incentives. Rather, they evolved personal skills and management practices for developing passion in others in regard to the success of the team and of the organization.

"My time and involvement with my church was very important to me. Our church is led by lay ministers (no paid pastors), and I have learned how to influence through non-financial means. I learned how to appeal, in a visceral sense, to the person someone wants to be. Everyone wants to be a winner and stand on the gold medal stand."

"Our company is as successful as we are today because of our people and the discretionary effort they exhibit every day . . ."

"My time in the military was invaluable. I learned that in pursuing a mission, people come first. Without people totally committed, we could not achieve our mission. That means that I had to earn the respect and trust of the people in my command and that they knew that I had their best interests at heart."

"Our company is as successful as we are today because of our people and the discretionary effort they exhibit every day. Our job as leaders is to unlock that—and to engage our workforce as fully as possible."

"It is important for me to have regular contact with all my direct reports and to commit a great deal of time to them. This is the one way I can truly get to know 'who' they are, 'what' they are thinking, and 'how' they are getting results. This includes providing them with informal, real-time feedback as well as taking the lead in initiating the formal review process."

2. Let Go of Things I Used to Do Well

Looking back over their career histories, the CEOs commented that as they progressed from one position to the next, they learned how to "let go" of those aspects of their previous job that they were good at and that they enjoyed. They found that they had to allow their successor to fulfill their old responsibilities and to remove themselves from many of the details of their previous role.

> *"In too many cases, the person in charge is expected to 'have all the answers and make all the decisions.' Instead, I discovered that when I focused on values and strategy, ensured that our employees understood both, and put the requisite tools, real-time information, and responsibility to act in their hands, productivity, results, and morale improved dramatically. Along the way I had to become comfortable with saying 'I don't know but I know where to find out.' CEOs and COOs who attempt to control everything and make most of the decisions create dysfunctional behaviors in themselves and in others, and fail to capture the productivity and creative capacity of their employees."*

> *"The contrast in the roles and the transition to CEO were difficult because I had to 'let go' of the things that I had done well in the past and that I personally enjoyed. I learned that I had to turn much of this over to others and then trust that my direct reports would do them well."*

> *"I learned that I must be able to change and become a different person. I had to develop and adopt behaviors that were different than the behaviors that brought me this far."*

3. Be Clear About the Behaviors and Competencies I Want to See in Others—and Serve as a Role Model

Many of the CEOs commented that one learning they brought with them to this role is the importance of being clear and explicit about the behaviors and competencies that they want to see and expect in others. These are the leadership behaviors that they want their senior team and other leaders to exhibit to one another and to the rest of the organization. They believe that these behaviors directly reflect the values and integrity of the company.

They also commented that it is not enough to tell people what is expected, but it is paramount that the senior executive, in this case the CEO, clearly exhibits these behaviors.

> *"I need to model the right behaviors, and I need to demand the right behaviors."*

> *"One thing I have learned is that it is important to be visible, and not just be visible but to exhibit the behaviors I expect from others. People are waiting to see what I do because what I do, not what I say, is what people believe is important. I need to model the right behaviors, and I need to demand the right behaviors."*

> *"Understand the sensitivities around whom you spend time with. You have to be very careful about the culture you create, unknowingly, simply by whom you spend time with."*

> *"One area that I feel was unique in my preparation for my serving as COO was my education and coaching in behavioral science. This exposure gave me an appreciation of the importance of values in leading an organization and the impact my own behaviors have in communicating what I believe is appropriate leadership. Together, the CEO and COO have to be in the forefront of exhibiting the values of the company, and they have to commit the resources to develop those same behaviors in others."*

"I spend a lot of time talking about core values and orchestrating initiatives instead of headcount."

"Surround yourself with people who are as good as, or better than, you are. You cannot win without outstanding talent around you whom you trust implicitly. You must have a common understanding of purpose that guides your work —and a common set of values that guides your behaviors and decisions."

"Surround yourself with people who are as good as, or better than, you are."

4. Be Clear and Relentless About Our Direction

In addition to being clear about the desired leadership behaviors, the participants in this study commented that they learned over the course of their careers that as they entered new and progressively more significant roles, it was important to be clear about their vision for the organization and the business direction. Not only must this vision and direction be clear, but it must be understandable and relentlessly communicated.

> *"I have learned how to engage people at various levels in the company and how to communicate an organization's strategy in a straightforward and understandable fashion, and more importantly, in a manner such that each person understands how his/her role contributes to that strategy."*

> *"I have also learned that I do not have to be charismatic to be effective; what I must have, however, is a vision and a relentless reservoir of energy and self-resolve to pursue the vision."*

> *"This comes down to paying attention to what people need to know, making sure the direction is clear, and giving them access to the information they need, but it also includes paying attention to them as individuals and letting them know they are valued. I have to pay attention to their heads and their hearts."*

> *"The new CEO coming into the role must believe in something, believe in what he/she wants to do. The CEO cannot simply believe in himself/herself, or simply believe in the power of the job. Rather, there needs to be a purpose—a mission to be pursued."*

"I also learned that I had to be relentless and boring in talking about and representing our values, and in talking about our strategic direction and reinforcing how our actions and decisions line up with our values and strategic direction..."

"I have also learned that I do not have to be charismatic to be effective; what I must have, however, is a vision and a relentless reservoir of energy and self-resolve to pursue the vision."

"I am glad that I prepared a vision early and communicated it as soon as I took the role of CEO. People needed to hear we were going to change, that we were going to be 'better,' and that their new CEO wanted to and could take them there. If I had not done this early in my tenure, I think the company would have continued in its present state and people would have begun to invent their own ideas of who the CEO is and what the company was all about. I should point out that in addition to having the vision, the CEO must be relentless in his or her commitment to it."

5. Provide Others with Timely Feedback and Acknowledgment

A management practice described by many of the CEOs is the delivery of real-time and fact-based feedback. This includes feedback that is intended to redirect another as well as feedback that is timely in acknowledging work well done.

"I estimate that I have spent somewhere between one-third and one-half of my time over the last 16 years on key people or at least on very people-intensive issues."

"I was able to coach, provide positive feedback, and demonstrate the desired behaviors I wanted and expected from others."

"When I have issues with my team, I call them in to discuss it immediately."

"People here work hard. Every day, people come here as though their job is the most important thing in the world. I want to encourage that spirit and keep it going. Our people are amazing."

"People here work hard. Every day, people come here as though their job is the most important thing in the world. I want to encourage that spirit and keep it going. Our people are amazing."

"The CEO must deal with and confront issues and people when they occur, and do it respectfully."

"It is important to have regular contact with all direct reports and spend a great deal of time with them. This is the one way the CEO and COO have to get to know 'who' they are. This includes providing them with informal, real-time feedback as well as taking the lead in initiating the formal review process."

"Hold your leaders accountable."

"We have a formal people development/management process that I spend a lot of time on. I make it my business to personally know our top 60–70 high potentials. I spend a lot of time discussing their strengths and weaknesses against key competencies we have defined. I have one-on-ones monthly with my direct reports, and I have one-on-one meetings once per year with each of our officers. These are informal times for us to just talk about things of importance to them or to me. I learn a lot from these conversations."

"I make it my business to personally know our top 60–70 high potentials."

6. Encourage Divergent Opinions

Many of the participants commented that they have developed skills and tools for prompting people to express divergent and challenging positions, and to challenge the CEO's thinking. As noted in the previous material, this is not an easy action for members of the senior team or for others, and it is incumbent on the CEO to devise his or her methods to encourage this healthful disagreement. In addition to prompting candor in others, many of the participants also indicated that they have found it equally important for them to be candid with their senior teams.

"The CEO's job is to create constructive tension."

"Those team members who wouldn't engage, I let them go. I needed people to shout and argue with me."

"Outside experiences have been a key to doing the job of CEO. They reinforced the importance of honest communications and candor in communications."

"I called the team back the next day and said I would like to revisit the decision. I also told them what I had heard (that they agreed with the original decision in the meeting but separately, in small groups, vigorously disagreed with the decision) and that if they were going to be on this team they would have to earn their position by being willing to tell me when they don't like something. I have done this a couple of times and it has helped us come together as a more effective team."

"Encourage your successor potentials to have their own points of view on things—and to develop their skills in expressing them well. CEOs are expected to have opinions on just about everything."

7. Assess and Act on Competency and Performance Issues

Almost all of the CEOs commented that it is important to act in a timely and prudent manner in regard to competency and performance issues. They further commented that during the course of their careers they have developed tools, resources, and skills intended to assess the talent around them.

> *"You cannot be successful unless you have an aligned team."*

> *"I watch body language. I won't tolerate passive-aggressive behavior."*

> *"I believe it is key to make things work with the team in place first AND get your team set for the long term. It's a delicate balance. You cannot be successful unless you have an aligned team."*

> *"Another area in which I have had a great deal of experience is in assessing and developing leadership talent. I am still getting to know some of the talent in the organization, but I can fairly quickly judge an individual's strengths and weaknesses and determine how they might be developed."*

> *"If you are not going to face and deal with the people issues . . . you have no business saying 'yes' to the job of CEO."*

> *"I think a big challenge of the CEO role is addressing different people's issues. If you are not going to face and deal with the people issues, I'd say you have no business saying 'yes' to the job of CEO."*

"In preparing to become CEO, it is essential to be highly effective in assessing, developing, shaping, and coaching others. It is also important to know how to bring talent into the organization. Finally, it is equally important to know when people should exit the organization."

"I changed out the entire leadership team, including our regional heads, marketing, HR, etc. I knew it was necessary in order to get the alignment and leadership behaviors we needed as a company."

"I have a 100-day rule-of-thumb."

"I have a 100-day rule-of-thumb. This is the time period during which change is easiest and people are most expecting it. In the first 100 days, I evaluate the level of talent in my staff and the value system of the senior team and other key positions. Once the evaluation is complete, I act to fix the gaps."

8. Use Candor in Communications

Another management practice that several of the CEOs described is the importance of honest and candid communications.

"I believe in complete candor. I have no hidden agendas."

"The great corporate myth is that what happens in the executive office is 'secret,' but in truth, employees and even external audiences 'worth their salt' are able to figure out what is occurring. It is better to be transparent and honest with this information than to continue to kid ourselves and believe it is hidden."

> *"I believe in complete candor. I have no hidden agendas."*

"I knew I had to address issues of trust and credibility on the part of employees in the company's leadership. One thing I did was immediately get in front of our employees and spoke candidly to them and did my best to make them feel like we were going to re-earn their trust."

"Outside experiences have been key to doing the job of CEO. They reinforced the importance of one's communications and candor in communications."

9. Collaborate

From past experience, many of the CEOs indicated that they learned the importance of collaboration with and within their senior team. They also discovered methods to help encourage this collaboration and brought these practices with them to the CEO role.

"A well-functioning team can overcome a lot of barriers. Teamwork and effective leadership by all is essential."

"Once I assumed my current role, I introduced a team development initiative to encourage greater collaboration and teamwork."

"Teaming by doing. People either get it or they don't get it."

"Having participated in team sports provides a strong sense of the value of the team and how the performance of the team is more important than the performance of individuals."

"Historically, we had been a highly collaborative company, sharing and shifting resources to meet client and market needs. But more recently, we had introduced major divisions with P&L's, and this has resulted in more competitive behavior and, in some cases, all-out battles. To a large extent this contributed to our weakening performance."

"A well-functioning team can overcome a lot of barriers. Teamwork and effective leadership by all is essential."

Summary

In summary, there was tremendous consistency and commonality around the attributes, experiences, and managerial practices of the participating CEOs that they felt were key to their success in the job. Part II has presented a treasure trove of information on what it takes to be a successful CEO, on what successful CEOs actually do, and what experiences were found to be most valuable in preparing for the job.

The CEO Handbook

PART III

AUTHOR
Leslie W. Braksick, Ph.D.
The Continuous Learning Group, Inc. (CLG)

CONTRIBUTING WRITER
Tracy Thurkow, Ph.D.
The Continuous Learning Group, Inc. (CLG)

THE CEO HANDBOOK

SEVEN

PREPARING WELL FOR THE JOB

The CEOs consistently stated that one of their discoveries when assuming the role was that fulfilling the core accountabilities of being CEO was not the hard part of the job. While the statement below came from one CEO, most of them offered the same sentiment, in their own words:

"I see that the job is not daunting."

The CEOs came to the helm ready to chart a course for the company, capable of making decisions and leading others. They were excited about the opportunity and felt honored to have been chosen to lead their respective organizations. There were surprises and learnings for all of them.

The surprises that most consistently challenged the study participants were the topics for the subsequent sections of this handbook, but they are not what you might first expect They are not about setting strategy or making decisions or refining their visions.

> *The surprises that most consistently challenged the study participants... are not what you might first expect.*

When asked what prepared them for the role of CEO, the study participants offered notably consistent perspectives as to the experiences that best prepared them for the job over the course of their careers. These experiences are the topic for this chapter.

In addition to these developmental experiences, many of the CEOs offered remarkably simple, yet profound, statements that guide them as CEOs.

"A CEO coming into the role must believe in something, believe in what she/he wants to do. The CEO cannot simply believe in herself/himself or simply believe in the power of the job."

"CEOs are expected to have opinions on just about everything. You need to be an opinion/thought leader, not a follower. Have a position on global warming, the economy, and the global financial situation."

"I discovered that when I focused on values and strategy, ensured that our employees understood both, and put the requisite tools, real-time information, and responsibility to act in their hands, productivity, results, and morale improved."

"I never want to hear, 'He didn't get results, but he did what you told him to do'."

"Be yourself."

"Never forget that in this job, you are only as good as your last quarter."

What are some experiences that many of the CEOs had in common and were described as integral to their preparation? Here's what the study participants had to say about the developmental experiences—both formal and informal—that prepared them for the job.

Study Highlights

While there is not a specific recipe for becoming CEO, the study participants reflected on the leadership assignments and experiences that they felt were key to their preparedness. They consistently identified the experiences described in this section as important.

Through these experiences and others, many of the study participants stated that they honed a handful of key skills throughout their careers that are essential to have as CEO. In essence, these skills are "table stakes" for becoming CEO. As one CEO said:

"I was able to do the strategic planning, business planning, the financial stuff, the communication strategy, working with leaders, and using team tools."

The foundational skills of setting strategy, executing strategy, and leveraging leadership talent are skills that candidates must possess in order to be an effective CEO.

Setting Strategy

Setting strategy was often an area in which the CEOs reported feeling comfortable. Identifying and choosing a "successful strategy" is key. In setting strategy, it is the CEO's job to be decisive and chart a course that they and others will stick to and follow.

"Based on my past experiences and assignments, I felt well-prepared to evaluate the company's overall strategy."

"I felt well-prepared to manage the business strategically. I knew what needed to be done to reposition the company in the industry through growth and acquisition, and to manage the enterprise's relationships with various national governments."

"Core accountabilities like capital allocation, resource deployment, strategy formulation, and leadership development are all learnable parts of the job. Those are the things I have learned to do over time. What are the most challenging are the soft things—these are harder to learn."

"Strategy skills are critical to being a successful CEO. Unfortunately, not all CEOs possess them. Strategy is not a 'learned skill.' You either have it or you don't."

"I felt that I was well-prepared to address issues of strategy, marketing, and branding, and in defining what success would look like. I also knew that I must engage a broad audience in the company in helping develop or influence the strategy. In fact, I expanded our existing strategic planning process to include up to 100 people."

"Set a bold agenda for the company, and drive to make it happen."

"The best piece of advice I got from my predecessor was there will be more opportunities to do more interesting things... and you will need to learn to say 'no.'"

"Whatever is the great theme of the day—such as globalization and technology—know it, and be prepared to succeed through it."

"Set a bold agenda for the company, and drive to make it happen. The agenda you develop comes from your past experience but requires courage to articulate. Strategy comes from experiential learning, bold moves, bold decisions, and sticking with what you decide. You may only have 50/50 buy-in at the time a decision gets made. But you must have the courage of conviction to still go with that decision and bring along the other 50%. Courage comes from watching others and trying, and pulling them up when they fail."

Orchestrating and Executing Strategy Through Others

Balancing the portfolio of the enterprise's offerings and enabling others to effectively execute unique business unit and product strategies is an essential skill for CEOs. Each put his/her individual fingerprints on the vision and direction of the company, and each knew it was something they had to be prepared to do when stepping into the role. They accepted ultimate accountability for the actions taken and the actions not taken, and for the outcomes that were realized and the outcomes not realized.

They also accepted ultimate accountability for the actions taken, not only by themselves, but also the actions and behaviors taken by their leadership teams.

"I am all about executing well through the people who report to me."

"As a result of the various roles I have held and the mentoring I received, I felt very well-prepared to focus on execution once we had agreed on our strategy."

"Intuition and courage are key to this position. You have to feel it and have a sense of prioritization to make things happen."

"The challenge is to leave your ego at the door. You have to have some, but we need to step back and keep the rest of the system running."

"My objective is to push authority back out into the operating units. This is my style."

"I was able to coach, provide positive feedback, and demonstrate the desired behaviors I wanted and expected of others."

"The buck stops with me … so, if you think something needs to be done, then change it. Anything that is not working well or right in the company is my responsibility. I can point no fingers."

Positioning and Leveraging Leadership Talent

Because a primary accountability of the CEO is ensuring the proper mix of leadership talent and then leveraging that talent to achieve the long-term goals of the enterprise, he/she must staff the organization with the best balance of leadership talent available. A key skill that the CEOs entered the job with is an ability to quickly assess the strengths and weaknesses of themselves and others and determine the optimal combination of leadership and technical competencies. Many of the CEOs reported that they regretted not moving faster to address leadership misfits or gaps when they existed.

"You can never have too good of a team. Upgrading the talent makes a magnitude of change in the organization. You probably never have a team as good as you think you have, and you can always improve your team."

"Another area I have had a good deal of experience in is assessing and developing leadership talent. I am still getting to know some of the talent in the organization, but I can fairly quickly judge an individual's strengths and weaknesses and determine how they might be developed."

"The CEO and COO must know who they are and their strengths and weaknesses. They must do this in an objective and introspective manner, and must often engage in some form of reality testing of their own self-assessments. By knowing their strengths, weaknesses, and blind spots, they can develop compensatory mechanisms. Without this knowledge, they cannot adequately compensate and, hence, cannot adequately lead."

"In preparing to become CEO, it is critical to be highly effective in assessing, developing, shaping, and coaching others. It is also important to know how to bring talent into the organization. Finally, it is equally important to know when people should exit the organization."

"If I had it to do over again, I would quickly determine the type of people I want on the leadership team and make sure I have those people. However, the team cannot be the 'CEO's team'— each team member must stand on his/her own virtue. It is true they need to be compatible with what the CEO needs, but they cannot be on the team because they agree with me or because I like them. On the contrary, I must tolerate people I do not like if they bring the right skills, values, and attitude."

"In the first 100 days, the CEO and COO should evaluate the level of talent and the value system in the senior team and in other key positions. Once the evaluation is complete, action should be taken on those who do not 'fit.'"

These experiences are explored in-depth in Detailed Findings in the next section, including:

1. International experience
2. Board exposure and experience
3. Running a business
4. Mentoring from boss and/or coach
5. Functional experience and/or business rotations
6. Use of leadership development resources and experiences

Detailed Findings

1. International Experience

The participating CEOs were nearly unanimous in identifying international experience as a prerequisite for the job. To them, international experience meant living and working outside the U.S.—traveling extensively was not enough. The CEOs felt that working and living internationally gave them important perspective about dealing with people, appreciating different cultures, and understanding how customers in other countries react to and interact with their company's products, services, pricing, and brand positioning.

The CEOs saw this experience as fundamental in today's global economy. One cannot lead a global company without knowing how to be a global citizen. Some went as far as to say that people who haven't lived and worked outside the U.S. are not qualified for the job.

"International experience is extremely important for the CEO of an international company like ours. It is important to understand global issues from a product standpoint and from the perspective of our customers."

"A lot of companies look at people as being knowledgeable if they know good English. People who have run businesses outside the U.S. don't think that way."

"Perhaps one of the most important positions I held was in an international setting. In this role I learned that there are commonalities in leadership across cultures. This is especially true in regard to the importance of treating people with respect and letting them know in different and multiple ways how much they are valued."

"I would not recommend anyone to succeed me who has not lived and worked overseas..."

"International experience is also critical in developing a much broader perspective in how other cultures work and think. This has helped me understand how different markets work and how people in different cultures are motivated."

"As a Chairman/CEO of this era, it is clear to me that we are moving away from being U.S. multinationals toward being truly global companies. They are so different."

"I would not recommend anyone to succeed me who has not lived and worked overseas. Living outside the U.S. develops different social interface capabilities; your brand means different things in different parts of the world, and customer expectations are different."

"Living and working in international settings was key. I had to learn different cultures, different cost structures, different ways of working. I spent five years in Europe and three years in Indonesia."

2. Board Exposure and Experience

Sitting CEOs consistently named Board experience as key. Board participation gave them experience with how Boards and CEOs work together—and how both play unique and different roles in governing the company. Having Board experience made them more comfortable with Board procedures, committee work, and other dimensions of how Boards operate. It also gave them an appreciation for the interpersonal dynamics of Boards and the importance of establishing good relationships with Board members. Beyond these benefits, participation on outside Boards gave the CEOs greater exposure to other organizations and their issues, which comforted them because they felt they "were not alone" and deepened their learning about how to deal with issues. Finally, some CEOs viewed outside Board participation as a way of giving back to their communities.

"I wish I had joined a publicly traded Board. I would have learned about interpersonal dynamics and parliamentary procedures."

"I am active on a number of other Boards, including for-profit and not-for-profit organizations. I find these to be important to me to keep me fresh and to provide me with an ever broader perspective on what other organizations are doing, but it is also a way of returning value to the various communities in which we operate or where we have influence."

"... I find these to be important to me to keep me fresh and to provide me with an ever broader perspective on what other organizations are doing."

"One thing that has been very helpful to me has been my participation on Boards of other companies. This participation requires a great deal of my time but it is well worth it. I am able to see how other companies operate, thus giving me a different perspective. More importantly, I can see that other companies are facing challenges similar to ours and that we are not alone."

"I had been an active and voting member of the Board for three years prior to becoming CEO. My predecessor had me presenting and discussing the state of the company during that time. As a result, I got to know the Board members and they got to know me. Governance is not a difficult part of the job."

> *"I had been an active and voting member of the Board for three years prior to becoming CEO. My predecessor had me presenting and discussing the state of the company during that time. As a result, I got to know the Board members and they got to know me."*

"One area that would have been helpful prior to becoming CEO would have been exposure to tools and ideas on establishing and managing relationships with the different personalities of the BOD members."

"I have been on the Boards of other companies for the past few years. This has enabled me to see how other companies and other Boards operate. They are much different than us, but they are equally successful. My participation on these Boards takes time, but it has been invaluable to see inside other companies and gain a different perspective."

"Clarity of the Board's responsibilities versus management's was a bit confusing at first. While I was quickly mentored on this, I was not clear about this at the outset."

3. Running a Business

Many of the CEOs in the study indicated that having had full P&L responsibility at some point in their career was a key stepping stone in their preparation. It allowed them to become comfortable operating the levers that drive a company's performance. It also enabled them to refine their skills in leading and integrating the efforts of other senior managers who represented a cross-section of organizational functions.

> *"You can't lead a business you don't understand. Understanding the business, honesty, and a commitment to lead well are the keys to being a great CEO."*

> *"My best preparation was running a real P&L with no costs from above, nothing fake."*

> *"The most important people in the organization are the frontline employees, the people that create and deliver value to the customer. The CEO should have some exposure to managing the core operating functions of the business. This way, the CEO will know what is truly important to the frontline employees. This will also develop credibility and trust between the CEO and the frontline. The candidate and the company should not be hesitant to rotate a VP through a GM role in order to provide this experience."*

> *"I had the opportunity to be the CEO of a smaller company. I ran a BU that had research, branding, etc., all of its own. That whole experience was invaluable in building my confidence and competence to run a large, global company."*

> *"You can't lead a business you don't understand. Understanding the business, honesty, and a commitment to lead well are the keys to being a great CEO."*

4. Mentoring from Boss and/or Coach

Learning by doing and by receiving feedback from a trusted source, be it a boss or an external coach, were key to preparing the CEOs. Underlying many of their comments was a consistent orientation toward learning and improving; the CEOs welcomed the opportunity to learn, to improve, and to fine-tune their leadership skills throughout their careers.

"I had excellent on-the-job training in these roles. My bosses were my best mentors, and I was able to make mistakes and learn along the way."

"I am a fan of informal versus formal mentoring ... people who didn't even know they were doing it. I also believe that external coaches can be very helpful. Feedback is key in any regard."

"It is not enough to be smart. To be effective the person in this role must have had practical experience in running a business."

"As a group executive, I worked directly with the Chairman and had many divisions reporting to me. Working hand-in-glove with our Chairman taught me much about his role and allowed him to teach me more about mine."

"I believe I don't know a lot of things, so I am a permanent student."

"It is not enough to be smart. To be effective the person in this role must have had practical experience in running a business."

"I had been working with an executive coach prior to becoming CEO, and this was particularly helpful... my coach helped me get into the mind of the other person and see life from his or her perspective. This helped me understand the root causes of their behavior and, as a result, I could see how I had to change my behavior to change theirs. I now try to truly understand other people and why they behave as they do."

"Thanks to my predecessor, I had been preparing myself for this role in one way or another for several years. Furthermore, we worked closely together during the last three years and he made sure that he counseled me in regard to what would be expected of me. In addition, he created opportunities for me to actually and meaningfully engage in and take responsibility for the activities that are associated with the role."

"I have people who I trust and turn to for feedback, insights, and advice. That includes some of my direct reports and others inside the company who are comfortable speaking directly with me and giving me advice. (I have to be willing to listen to their feedback and advice.) I also talk with my predecessor a lot. He's a good sounding board for me, and while we don't always agree on things, I find the conversations very helpful."

"Not only did my predecessor prepare me for the role, he also helped prepare my wife. During the three years prior to my becoming CEO, he would make a point of sitting next to my wife on social occasions and use this time to talk to her about what it would mean to her and to our family once I took this role. It scared her half to death but she was prepared in some ways she would not otherwise be."

5. FUNCTIONAL EXPERIENCE AND/OR BUSINESS ROTATIONS

The CEOs felt depth and breadth of experience in the business was key to their development. In part, this experience provided them with functional depth. It also provided them with a greater appreciation for how to relate to and lead people with different backgrounds and roles in the business.

"I believe that to be effective, the CEO must have some foundational skill, one that the CEO is particularly good at. Mine is in marketing and brand management, but it could be in finance or some other area."

"I was very fortunate in the positions I have held in other organizations. These positions have played a significant role in preparing me for my current position. I have been in major sales positions, I have been in a marketing role, and I have been in operations. In these roles I have learned how to engage people at various levels in the company and how to communicate an organization's strategy in a straightforward and understandable fashion and, more importantly, in a manner such that each person understands how his or her role contributes to that strategy."

---

6. Use of Leadership Development Resources and Experiences

Many of the CEOs reported that they sought resources to support their own leadership development. These resources ranged from reading to executive development classes to seeking an executive coach.

"Over the past 25 or more years, I have read many business articles and thought pieces, including practically every HBR issue. I don't think I can quote any specific model from all of these readings, but collectively they have given me a framework in which to view and understand many of the challenges I am facing."

"I went to a Harvard four-day class for new CEOs run by Porter. He talked a lot about, 'What do you want them to write about you when you leave?' That really stuck with me and has helped to ground me throughout."

"I went to a Harvard four-day class for new CEOs run by Porter. He talked a lot about, 'What do you want them to write about you when you leave?' That really stuck with me and has helped to ground me throughout."

"I worked with a consultant as part of a 'Great Leaders Program.' He gave me some great articles on the different stature you have as CEO, internally and externally."

Recommendations

As our study participants pointed out, there is no one path to becoming CEO. That said, there are a number of common experiences that were consistently identified as key to their preparedness.

Some of these experiences naturally come with the assignments that a person on the path to becoming CEO is likely to take on. People who demonstrate executive skills—the ability to lead, grow a business—are likely to be promoted into executive positions. These roles are likely to give them international experience, put them in front of the Board for business reviews, and give them P&L responsibility for increasingly larger parts of the organization.

> *I am in a position to learn quickly. Good leaders orchestrate that fast-paced learning."*

Of course, not everyone who has these experiences will become CEO. While it is interesting to speculate on what distinguishes these CEOs from candidates who were not named to the job, this study does not specifically address those differences.

However, a theme underlying many of the study participants' comments is that they actively sought experiences throughout their careers, including in their role as CEO, that stretched their own thinking and caused them to "up their game." They sought and capitalized on many different opportunities to hone their skills and sharpen their thinking.

"We all get better by taking a few learnings and truly applying them."

"I think that an effective CEO will have demonstrated that he/she is sincerely interested in continuous self-development."

"I continuously learn to keep my curiosity on fire."

"I am in a position to learn quickly. Good leaders orchestrate that fast-paced learning."

If you are interested in becoming CEO, you might or might not know if you are considered a candidate for the job in your company, depending on your company's succession planning practices. However, there are a number of learnings that you can glean from the study participants to take charge of your own development. Doing so might better position you for the top job in your current company; it might also open opportunities for you at another company.

1. Career Development Experiences

International Experience

- Seek out and/or accept an opportunity to live and work overseas. While there was no prescribed duration for working overseas, almost every CEO pointed to at least one, if not several, overseas assignments that were key to their development.

- When working overseas, use the opportunity to deepen your understanding of what it takes for your business to succeed. How do different people from different cultures react to your products and services and your brand proposition? How do they define value, and what does that mean for you? What unique regulatory requirements do you face? What pricing pressures do you face?

- What is it like to be in a business setting where you are the ethnic minority? How do you cultivate the relationships that you need in order to lead your business more effectively?

- How do you learn more about the culture? How do you become accepted into the culture? What practices are frowned upon? How do you help your family adapt?

- Also, when working overseas, hone your perspective about what it means to be a leader. What does a leader need to do to relate to people from different backgrounds and cultures? Are there commonalities to leadership across cultures? What leadership behaviors are culturally unique? What does it take to establish credibility and trust? How do they define your success?

Board Exposure and Experience

- Seek out opportunities to serve on one or more Boards. Some CEOs reported finding non-profit Boards helpful; the majority of CEOs reported that sitting on the Board for a publicly traded company was important.

- Pay attention to parliamentary procedures, committee structures, and responsibilities of Board members. Pay particular attention to what a CEO is accountable to the Board for delivering.

- Pay particular attention to the boundaries between Board oversight and management responsibilities. Note what happens when these boundaries are unclear or are crossed.

- Consider the mix of talent that exists on a Board. Who is on the Board and why? What value does each individual add? What is missing?

- Take the opportunity to observe the importance of developing relationships with Board members in order to facilitate the Board's effective operations. How effectively does the Board work when the interpersonal relationships are healthy? How effectively does the Board work when the interpersonal relationships are strained? What does it take to improve interpersonal relationships with Board members?

Running a Business

- Seek opportunities to take on P&L responsibility for increasingly larger and more complex organizational units. Use those opportunities to become comfortable making decisions with increasingly significant financial and cultural implications. Consider keeping a journal to capture the lessons you learn, both through your successes and your failures.

- As you make decisions for your portion of the business, take the CEO's perspective. Ask yourself, how will decisions I make impact the enterprise as a whole? Based on the results the CEO is trying to achieve, does my decision help or hurt his/her strategy? Talk with the CEO or other senior leaders to compare your points of view.

- Be clear on the profit drivers for your business and for the company. Understand where money is made and spent—and how the various parts of the company portfolio add up to the whole.

Functional Experience and/or Business Rotations

- Many of the study participants advocated having both functional depth in at least one area as well as a working understanding and appreciation for the other business functions and, in particular, the interrelationships among the various functions.

- First, make sure you are a high performer in your chosen functional area. Build your credibility and track record. As you do so, make sure you work well with other functional leaders and come to appreciate the expertise they bring to the organization. It will be important for you to build your track record as a collaborative functional leader.

- Beyond collaborating with functional leaders, develop your skills for leading other functional leaders. Seek opportunities as a general manager to give you experience leading people running other functions. You will hone your skills delegating and deferring to other experts while at the same time providing overall direction, making tradeoff decisions across functions, and holding leaders accountable for performance in areas where you are not a technical expert.

- Learn new functions that are not in your core area of expertise by spending more time in these areas when you are running your own P&L. Understand the value of these functions and what their measures of success are. Be sure to fully understand the issues of finance, marketing, sales, research and development, supply chain, and human resources.

2. Investor and Market Analyst Relations

An area identified by many of the CEOs as critical to early success in the role was the ability to present to, dialogue with, and manage investors and market analysts. In preparation for the role of CEO, request coaching from your current CEO on how he/she approaches analyst/investor calls—and ask to be part of the planning/preparation conversations. Listen to and read transcripts from investor and analyst meetings from other companies. Write down your learnings and observations. Seek time with your internal head of Investor Relations. Learn the issues impacting your business' sector and who is taking what position.

3. Seek Coaching and Mentoring, Build Self-Awareness

Mentoring from Boss and/or Coach

- As you move up in the organization, chances are that you will receive less and less objective feedback about your impact and performance. Just as professional athletes, artists, and other premiere performers seek out coaches to provide them with an objective assessment and feedback, and to explore options for overcoming shortcomings, engage one or more trusted advisors to do this for you. They will need to be able to see you in action as well as talk with others about the impact of your performance on them. You can seek mentors internal to the organization and/or retain an external coach.

- Self-awareness was identified as one of the critical underlying personal attributes by the CEOs. Mentoring, coaching, and feedback early in your career and continuing into the executive suite can serve you well. Everyone is self-aware to some degree, but everyone also has "blind spots," especially as you find yourself in new situations. The CEOs described the importance of continual self-evaluation as well as candid feedback from others. You have to know your blind spots in order to overcome them or compensate for them.

Use of Leadership Development Resources and Experiences

- Consider whether there are specific areas in which you would like to enhance your leadership skills. There are many good leadership development programs available either internally (in some organizations, but not all) and externally. Many of the renowned business schools have executive education programs.

- Take advantage of books and publications targeted specifically for executives. Read them and consider whether they offer you ideas you can put into practice. Consider establishing a discussion group with your peers inside or outside the organization to explore recent publications; if you choose to work with an executive coach, you can also work with your coach to debrief and apply your learnings.

4. Personal Values

Many of the CEOs were able to "list" the values they had discovered over the course of their careers that they found to be important in managing relationships and in leading others. They were able to describe the values, but more importantly, were able to describe the behaviors that comprised each of those values. Further, they were able to describe incidents when they displayed those same behaviors and when they did not. They brought these values with them and have used them to define their own code of conduct and the code of conduct they want from their senior team. In preparing for the position, it will be important for you to define the values you believe are important, behavioralize them, and then continually and honestly assess your own day-to-day behavior in relation to those values. You will truly be known by what you do and not what you say.

Attributes/qualities you need to have to be a successful CEO in this globally challenging era:

"Integrity, high standards, credibility with people. People need to believe you are doing the right/best thing for the organization and not furthering your own self-interests."

"Be willing to make choices and decisions without knowledge about everything you want to know. You need to have the ability to understand what choices need to be made and what don't."

"Be willing to try and fail. My biggest learnings along the way have come when I have tried and failed—especially when it is something that I really believed in and thought would work. You have to be willing to learn and to accept feedback and advice from others. It is key to your continuous growth and improvement."

"Be able to listen and learn. Everyone assumes the CEO has all of the answers. Usually that is not the case. Push yourself to keep on learning. Listen before you speak up in a meeting."

---

5. Prepare for and Take Advantage of the First 100 Days

You never get a second chance to make a first impression, so the saying goes. The first 90 to 100 days in your new job as CEO are critical. It is during this period that you have access to people and information that you might not have again as you ask questions to determine what you need to learn about the organization. It is also during this period that people learn and understand your agenda and who you are. They form lasting opinions of you as a leader. Begin mapping out the skeleton of your 100-day plan as soon as you learn you are a serious candidate for the position. Sharing this information may be helpful in your interview process with the Board.

"My first days, I was so exhausted and I had no plan. I was so busy lining up my old job, completing my to-do list. I was so busy wanting to turn in good results in my division. Just focus on the first 100 days in your new job and new role. Your successor will take care of the rest in your old job."

"The honeymoon period is absolutely vital. Internal candidates think they know the organization, and think that the organization knows them, but this is a big mistake."

"Get an executive coach to help you make the transition… to discuss problems with you and to problem-solve around things such as the interpersonal challenges of managing former peers."

EIGHT

The Handoff from the Previous Chairman/CEO

The handoff from one CEO to the next is a particularly important time, not only for the individuals involved, but for the organization. A change in leadership brings other changes, sometimes welcomed and sometimes feared. How the transition period is handled can influence the early days of a new CEO's tenure. In general, it is key to acknowledge the successes of your predecessor and to respect the past, while clearly building upon it in new ways.

Study Highlights

Nearly all of the CEOs in the study reported that they inherited a strong company. All of the CEOs reported that they were prepared for and eager to step into the leadership role and felt as though they had clear perspectives about what it would take to lead the company to success.

Many of the CEOs reflected on how well the baton was passed by their predecessor. In some cases, the relationship between departing and incoming CEOs was smooth and helpful, enabling the transition to occur more naturally. In other cases, the transition was strained and could not happen fast enough for one party or for both. The transition dynamics also influenced how quickly the new CEO was able to cultivate constructive working relationships with the Board, particularly when the departing CEO stayed on as chairman.

The CEOs' experiences and comments are presented in the next section, Detailed Findings, in these categories:

1. **Changing market and external environment**
2. **Challenges from inside**
3. **Interpersonal/relationship dynamics in the handoff**
4. **What worked/what I wish had been different about the transition**

Detailed Findings

1. Changing Market and External Environment

The study participants commented on the market and competitive conditions that led them to define their first strategic steps as CEO.

"The business was great. It was strong and healthy. My predecessor was a good CEO and managed it well. We faced significant headwinds in the market and regulatory environment that we needed to address."

"I came in with an argument that we could perform at higher rates than what we had been... and that I wanted us to perform better. This was a core bet of mine. Winning today gives you no certainty of winning tomorrow."

"The organization just came off the '90s boom, and we needed to change. We were in a down market and we needed fewer brands and tremendous focus. Companies in our space were consolidating. Therefore, we needed to consolidate our brands. This required radical changes in our strategy and in our culture that were tough on the organization."

"From a market position, we were falling behind strategically in that competitors were becoming much larger, primarily through acquisition."

"Early in my tenure, I was determined to reset the culture and the company's moral compass, balancing the achievement of business results with continuous and steady effort in establishing the type of culture I believed would position the company for the long-term."

"The business was in very good condition. I took over at the end of a bubble economy. At the same time, Enron was unraveling. This was right after 9/11."

"I knew that although we were in solid shape for the time and had a well-thought-out strategy, we were entering a new era and our current strategy was too narrow as we anticipated what we saw unfolding in the future. I believed we were too narrow in terms of our product offerings and we were too narrow in our geographic focus. We were trapped within our own categories and, in effect, had to reconfigure our portfolio, which we proceeded to do."

"When I became CEO, we had gone through a difficult time for the company. We were in a contentious relationship with the government and regulators."

"When I became CEO, the company had gone through a great deal of turmoil. The Chairman and CEO had retired and we had experienced overall poor performance, resulting in a decline in our stock price. In addition, business in general was under scrutiny because, at the time I became CEO, the problems with Enron and WorldCom were becoming known."

"As I assumed the role, I saw two major opportunities. The company was lagging its competitors in changes that had been prevalent in the marketplace for some time. For example, our competitors had taken advantage of offshore operations. The second opportunity had to do with our restructuring. We had not restructured our base business and how we approached the marketplace. I knew we now had to address these issues."

"Prior to my joining the company, my sense was that it was running out of steam. There were signals that things were not going well several months before I joined."

"I followed a predecessor who had been in the role for well over a decade… and was well-known in our industry, as well as throughout other industries and with government officials. He had watched our industry go through dramatic changes and had engineered a highly successful course for our company. During the past few years we have made some significant acquisitions and positioned ourselves as the largest provider of services and products… however, the current economic conditions and business climate have impacted us and our stock price is down significantly."

"I knew that although we were in solid shape for the time and had a well-thought-out strategy, we were entering a new era and our current strategy was too narrow as we anticipated what we saw unfolding in the future."

"When I became CEO, I was following a CEO who had been in the position for seven years. The business was doing okay, but not great. We had just completed a sizeable number of acquisitions with mixed success. Performance had improved, but not a lot, and the world around us was changing quickly. We thought we had a good strategy—but it became apparent fairly quickly that the status quo was not even going to keep us even. We needed a new strategy without the benefit of a real burning platform other than that we weren't satisfied with being a little better than average."

"It took almost two years before we had a plan and the buy-in/approval of that plan across senior management and with our Board. It was a transformative plan for our company, and it took a lot of time to get everyone on board with it. This was all happening as significant turnover was occurring on our Board. Nine of our ten Board members are different today than when I became CEO."

2. Challenges from Inside

Some study participants identified challenges inside the company that guided their strategies as CEO.

"When I joined, I thought I had done my due diligence well. I did a lot of research on the company and met with the Board and with senior management. Once I assumed the role of CEO, however, I found the company to be in more problematic shape than I anticipated. The company did not have a clear and unifying vision, and it became evident to me that employees at all levels were anxious to have one; they wanted to know where the company was headed in the future. I also found that I had to insert myself into the business. I think if I had not taken the initiative, I could have stayed in my office and waited for others to reach out to me, but if I had done this, I don't think the phone would have rung nor would I have received any e-mails."

"The more I studied the issues around growth, the more I realized that we must shift our focus to our portfolio of products and to the geographies in which we operate."

"The business was not in as good a shape as I had thought. I had thought that what we needed was a clearer focus, a long-term strategy, and a more performance-oriented culture. What I learned very quickly was that we were almost in a 'turnaround' situation."

"We suffered from lack of identity and clarity on who we wanted to be. The company related as a holding company but didn't provide integration value."

"My predecessor did not reinvest as much as the company needed. He focused more on over-delivering profits. As I look ahead, profit and continued growth require bold moves."

"The culture was driven on fear—'What do we need to do to survive?'"

"This is a company that has grown tremendously over the past 100 years. It grew through three acquisitions primarily. It had legendary leaders. I was surprised by the high degree of fear and mistrust. I didn't realize how hurt this company was by things in its past and how betrayed people felt. I was also surprised at how long it took, especially bringing together the new members and the old members."

"Although the business was healthy and had a solid balance sheet, growth had begun to slow. The more I studied the issues around growth, the more I realized that we must shift our focus to our portfolio of products and to the geographies in which we operate. I found that the company was fairly cautious and conservative in its approach to decisions and to taking risks. Further, the definition of 'success' was not clear. We had a lot of measures but no one, unifying objective."

"When I became CEO, times were good and there was a temptation to add to headcount as well as expand other resources. Everything folks were bringing forward sounded like a good idea… and it generally meant they needed additional people to do it with. As CEO, I had to recognize that this was a potential trap and that I owned putting tight limits on spending and adding to headcount. There is simply no one for the CEO to buck it up to. I had to get comfortable with doing this."

"At the time I became CEO, I concluded that we were behind the times in regard to our management practices. We had not focused on our culture, and we had a miserable 30% approval rating by our customers and the public."

"I knew that we did not have the ability to act as one company. It was not that we did not have good people. Rather, we worked in highly insulated silos."

3. Interpersonal/Relationship Dynamics in the Handoff

The CEOs in the study commented on the interpersonal dynamics between themselves and their predecessors during the handoff. The nature of those dynamics ran the gamut between working well to being painful and awkward.

"My predecessor stayed on for 18 months; it was much too long. I wish it had been handed off differently."

"When I stepped in as CEO, he was the Chairman of the Board. It was his Board. Any change I introduced was reflected as criticism of him."

"My predecessor was a wonderful human being, but we didn't agree a lot."

"My predecessor stayed on for 18 months; it was much too long."

"My predecessor has been extremely helpful. He has bitten his lip even when he disagreed with the direction in which I wanted to take the organization."

"Personally, I thought it went reasonably well."

"I was President/COO for one year. The businesses reported to me; I was also on the Board. My predecessor remained in control of HR, Finance, and IT for one year. Soon thereafter, in my role as President, COO, and Board member, I was making the presentations to the analysts and became the main spokesperson to the analyst's community."

"The last two Chairman changeouts were abrupt. There was little overlap between the outgoing person and incoming person."

"My predecessor didn't want to be a lame duck. He was Chairman until mid-month when I was appointed, and then the next day he stepped aside."

"My predecessor stepped out suddenly—just didn't want to do the job anymore."

"Once the successor is known, the time of overlap between the retiring CEO and the incoming CEO should be relatively short —three to four months. It will need to be clear who is in charge, and a longer overlap can become confusing to the organization and hamper the new CEO in regard to implementing changes."

"Once the successor is known, the time of overlap between the retiring CEO and the incoming CEO should be relatively short— three to four months."

"We worked closely together during the last three years and he made sure he counseled me in regard to what would be expected of me… The movement into the role was as natural as any other career steps I had taken."

4. WHAT WORKED/WHAT I WISH HAD BEEN DIFFERENT ABOUT THE TRANSITION

Many of the CEOs commented on what they learned during the transition period. In some cases, they noted areas that would have helped them make the transition happen more smoothly or set them up to be effective more quickly when they assumed the job.

"It would have been helpful to have had a better assessment of the individuals on the senior management team at the time I became CEO. I was surprised that members of the team were weaker than I had assumed, and I inherited underperformers. Because I was not aware of some of these weaknesses, it took a while (approximately two years) to assess and realign the team and, hence, to implement some of the changes in strategy and execution."

"It would have been helpful to have had a better assessment of the individuals on the senior management team at the time I became CEO. I was surprised that members of the team were weaker than I had assumed, and I inherited underperformers."

"Some residual issues I have to address are special arrangements my predecessor had made with different people. He was a loyal individual, and when someone went out of his/her way to help the company in some way, my predecessor wanted to make sure that person was helped in return. Therefore, we have some people internally and some business ties with people outside the company that don't make sense right now. I believe that I have to address them and do this in a way that treats them with dignity and does not tarnish my predecessor's legacy."

Some of the CEOs wished they had learned more about the organization and its people before stepping into the role.

"I had a chance to meet with senior management before I became CEO, but I did not have an opportunity to meet with lower levels of management. As a result, I heard the senior team's description of the company's culture, but after I joined the company and began to meet with mid-management in informal discussions, I learned a great deal more, and often what I learned was much different than I had thought based on my conversations with the senior team members."

"I also wish I had had an opportunity to talk with some of our major customers. I knew we had some issues, but I did not realize how grave some of those issues were. I do not believe anyone was misleading me or withholding information—I think people did not know the depth of some of these issues."

"He was Executive Chairman for six months and non-Executive Chairman for one year. That was extremely helpful for me as I was not, then, overlapping with him for BOD leadership. He handled the BOD but retired when we did the merger so there was no overlap in the 'combined company.' During the period that he was Chairman and I was CEO, I would give him a monthly update, and he would take me to investor meetings so I could be mentored in that process without owning it entirely."

"Our compensation system for senior executives was not designed well. It did not have the leverage built into it that is often important in providing direction and motivation for executives."

"There is not too much that I did not know when I joined the company, but there were some things I was able to do before I joined and during the first few months of my tenure to understand what the company's culture was like."

"I realized that you never know as much as you think you know."

Some of the CEOs reported that they would have liked more contact and communication with the departing CEO.

"I would have liked to have one day a week with the prior CEO to talk about 'stuff that mattered'…I would have liked to have had feedback on what I was doing and how well I was doing it. I would have liked to have had counsel on how to work with the Board and how to repair rifts among Board members, and to create alignment among individuals with multiple agendas and objectives."

"There really was not much overlap. It was not ideal from my standpoint. I would have much preferred for us to have traveled together, to have had him introduce me to other CEOs, etc. I didn't need a lot of time, but a more orderly and complete handing over would have been helpful."

"There really was not much overlap. It was not ideal from my standpoint. I would have much preferred for us to have traveled together, to have had him introduce me to other CEOs, etc. I didn't need a lot of time, but a more orderly and complete handing over would have been helpful."

Recommendations

While no firm recommendations came forward from the study about how long a handoff should last or what the departing and incoming CEOs should do or say during the handoff, a consistent theme did emerge. Without question, the CEO transition should be done first and foremost with the needs of the organization and the shareholders front and center. It is important that you build upon the successes of what your predecessor did and enable his/her transition out of the CEO role to be a graceful one.

Often the timetable and desires of the outgoing Chairman/CEO factor heavily into issues of timing and overlap. Regardless of how the transition is sequenced, the relationship between the departing and incoming CEOs is a critical success factor in the handoff process, as is their mutual effort to meet each other's needs during the transition. Take the high road. Recognize that different times require different leaders. Do everything you can to ensure there is a smooth and positive transition between you and your predecessor.

The health of the relationship between the new CEO and his/her predecessor depends, in part, on the extent to which there is a clear delineation of accountabilities. The new CEO must enter the relationship as his or her own person with a clear vision and near-term concrete steps. The retiring CEO has a similar and perhaps greater responsibility in setting aside a personal investment in his or her legacy and entering into an objective and collaborative dialogue with the new CEO.

From the standpoint of role clarity, the retiring CEO must also recognize that the new CEO is "running the company."

As the incoming CEO, you will find yourself eager to step forward as the company's new leader and begin meeting with people and traveling to your various sites. As we have mentioned many times, these first 100 days are key. It is also important, however, to attend to your relationship with your predecessor, particularly if he/she will continue as Chairman of the Board. Your first 100 days should include things like:

- Learning as much information as you can about the individuals on the senior team, about the health of the business, about how the Board is working, and so on

- Introducing yourself to top executives of key customers, other CEOs, Board members, and key members of the analyst community and governmental bodies

- Beginning to communicate with the organization about your vision and values

- Ensuring clarity of direction as you help to create momentum around the performance and future of the company

- Modeling the teamwork you seek from others by inviting input; asking others for their point of view; crediting others openly for their good work; modeling the use of collaboration

- Beginning to assess the caliber of talent around you so you can either change the people or change the people

- Actively listening to people all across the company and communicating often; spending considerable time upfront visiting sites and talking with customers, employees, suppliers, etc.

- Writing, delivering, and sending personalized communications praising good work and progress; sharing your view on information in the news and how it affects the organization; providing positive feedback/praise for good work being done inside the company that can be shared with a broader audience than you will personally come in contact with.

Also recall that your predecessor will have distinct needs such as:

- Having his or her contributions to the organization recognized and celebrated by you and others—through your words and actions

- Having you respect and value information and/or insights he/she offers in the spirit of setting you up for success

- Clarifying what he/she will do as Chairman (if staying in that role) and what you will do as CEO, particularly as it relates to leadership and communications with the Board

Healthy communication between you and your predecessor is key for all parties. As you find the demands for your time and attention multiplying, be sure to set aside time for important business and personal discussions with your predecessor. Many have found it helpful to occasionally meet with their predecessor to have a sounding board who understands and can help think through various options and consequences.

Finally, having a plan to guide your first 100 days is essential to leveraging that once-in-a-lifetime window of time with the organization and people you have just inherited. Don't let that window close. Engineer it to get you off to the best possible start as the new CEO of your company!

NINE

LEADING YOUR NEW TEAM

The CEO study participants were emphatic and passionate about their commitment to people. A CEO's success is so visibly dependent on the success of the people around him/her that the person holding the job must make working effectively with and through others a top priority. It is the team's ability to execute what will ultimately define the CEO's success and, hence, the success of the enterprise.

"People are number one. They are the most important and the most challenging issues."

"Critical to my success is that one-third of my time is spent working with people. I worked hard at this as I was coming up through the company."

"I think a big challenge of the CEO role is addressing different people's issues. If you are not going to face into and deal with the people issues, I'd say you have no business saying 'yes' to the CEO job."

"Be sure you get the best out of all of the people you work with."

"I am all about executing well through the people who report to me."

"Most of what I actually do as CEO is through our key leadership team. I would estimate that well over one-half my influence is through eight people or fewer, another one-fourth is through the next 35, and the last one-fourth is more widely dispersed across thousands of folks, including employees of all levels, customers, suppliers, and important other constituents."

"Leadership roles at our level are to help others succeed."

"Collaboratively shaping the senior leadership team like this is critical because CEO succession is really executive suite succession."

"My executives are people first, company executives second. I want to connect with them as people and as company executives."

The CEOs also expressed that they profoundly felt accountability for providing effective leadership and role modeling to their people. They hold themselves to high standards when it comes to being a leader that their people trust and respect. This includes recognition that their employees are people first and company executives/employees second.

"People need and deserve great leadership—which is different than what it looked like in the past."

"This comes down to paying attention to what people need to know, making sure the direction is clear, and giving them access to the information they need—but it also includes paying attention to them as individuals and letting them know they are valued. I have to pay attention to their heads and their hearts."

"I send correspondence to parents and spouses of my executive team. This is very important to me."

"Although I knew it was going to be difficult and I wasn't sure how I was going to do it, I knew I had to address issues of trust and credibility on the part of employees in the company's leadership."

"A well-functioning team can overcome a lot of barriers. Teamwork and effective leadership by all is essential."

"I knew that to attend to people's hearts and heads, I and the senior team must work from an inverted organizational pyramid. The position of senior leadership is at the bottom of the pyramid, and our role is to enable others to perform and to remove obstacles for them."

"Most of what I actually do as CEO is through our key leadership team."

"My executives are people first, executives second. I want to connect with them as people and as company executives. I went all over the world to meet with the parents of my direct reports, and those travels will continue. It is a high priority for me."

The CEOs also were quite clear about their commitment to developing their leadership team. They expressed a sincere need for their leadership team to function as a team, not merely as a group of talented individuals. Given the complexities of not only operating, but succeeding, in today's world, a highly effective team is considered a "must have."

"The complexity of today's business world is far beyond what one person can handle. You need a great team to win."

"I learned that I was not 'in control.' I could not effectively control all decisions and actions in the company. To be effective, I had to push decisions and the ability to influence out to my staff. CEOs and COOs who attempt to control everything create dysfunctional behaviors in others and an organization that is not sustainable."

Study Highlights

Given their adamant focus on cultivating people and their teams, it is not surprising that the CEOs in the study reported spending significant time and energy on "people issues." The study participants shared their learnings in the areas of selecting, aligning, developing, and leading their senior teams. In some cases, the CEOs faced particularly sensitive situations, like leading former peers (some of whom were also candidates for the CEO job), dealing with performance issues left unaddressed by their predecessors, or entering into an organization for the first time and needing to establish rapport with the team while assessing their fit going forward.

> *"In preparing to become CEO, it is critical to be highly effective in assessing, developing, shaping, and coaching others. It is also important to know how to bring talent into the organization. Finally, it is equally important to know when people should exit the organization."*

In addition, the CEOs shared their perspectives on what is required of them as leaders once they are in the CEO role. They shared how they had to elevate themselves from old patterns of behavior that were comfortable and effective for them in previous roles.

> *"Operational executives are a dime a dozen. I have three outstanding COOs and the business needs them, but they don't need me to be the fourth."*

> *"Imagine a large enterprise similar to the Catholic Church. My move up was like becoming cardinal. Becoming a cardinal affects how you think of yourself, how you operate or maintain within an existing environment versus a changing environment."*

> *"When a person steps up as CEO, a person has to move away from the day-to-day business and have confidence in the people in place. This is not a transition that happens overnight."*

"As CEO, I quickly learned that I must act dispassionately and objectively in my relationships with people and that I must make decisions about people and about business units that potentially conflicted with old loyalties."

"Among the most significant challenges for me was dealing with the differences between the role of the COO and the role of the CEO. As COO, I dealt with tangible and measurable issues, built and capitalized on interpersonal relationships, acted as an organizational 'cheerleader,' delegated tangible responsibilities with measurable outcomes, and tackled specific business operating issues."

"The role of CEO is both the most powerful and the least powerful job in the company. The CEO is charged with managing and leading the enterprise but simultaneously is subject to review and critique by numerous 'bosses.' Further, the CEO frequently lacks objective, real-time data to determine whether what he/she wants done or expects to be done is actually getting done."

The CEOs also demonstrated a remarkable humility, often downplaying their individual contributions to the organization and emphasizing their obligation to ensure others' success.

"As CEO, I get more attention than I need or than is good for anyone. It is key that we go out of our way to spotlight others, relinquish credit/ownership to others. They are our future."

"People here work hard. We don't save lives. We make simple pleasures of life. Yet, every day people come here as though their job is the most important thing in the world. I want to encourage that spirit and keep it going. Our people are amazing."

"People can make you feel like you are a king. Don't be deluded into believing that or them."

The CEOs' experiences and comments are detailed in the following section, in these categories:

1. Selecting the senior team
2. Acting on talent gaps or issues
3. Leading former peers
4. Leading the team when joining as a CEO from the outside
5. Aligning the senior team
6. Developing leadership talent

Detailed Findings

1. Selecting the Senior Team

One of the first jobs of a new CEO is to select his or her senior team. The study participants commented extensively on the importance of not compromising on the effectiveness of the leadership team. In some cases, it was a delicate balance to work with in-place leaders while bringing in and/or replacing some leaders to increase the team's capability.

"Make your key hires early on..."

"You can never have too good of a team. Upgrading the talent makes a magnitude of change in the organization. You probably never have a team as good as you think you have, and you can always improve your team."

"I believe it is key to make things work with the team in place first AND get your team set for the long-term. It's a delicate balance."

"I have a 100-day rule. In the first 100 days, the CEO and COO should evaluate the level of talent and the value system in the senior team and in other key positions. Once the evaluation is complete, action should be taken on those who do not 'fit.'"

"I gave everyone six months. I was wonderful to everyone, and worked closely to help and support them. No one left me feeling badly."

"The beauty of my pathway to CEO (coming in to lead at the time of a major merger) was that I had to build a new leadership team. It gave me the confidence that I could bring my team together, and I used an outside consultant to help me."

"Make your key hires early on. I brought in a communications person and a new HR lead and they continue to be key to the new culture we are creating here."

"During the three years prior to becoming CEO, my predecessor and I worked closely in reviewing all of our key executive talent. As the time neared for me to move into the role, my predecessor began addressing many of the talent and style issues. Where appropriate, he helped them exit with grace and dignity. In the meantime, I was able to identify who I wanted in key positions and, over three or so years, began to orchestrate their development so they would be ready to step up when I entered the role. As a result, I had my team pretty much in place when I took the job."

"I made several changes in the leadership of the company but I knew I was going to have to do that. Some were good and some were not. The important thing is to screen people based on performance and not on their relationships."

2. Acting on Talent Gaps or Issues

More often than not, when new CEOs assessed the talent on their senior team, they identified talent gaps or issues. While some considered it a difficult situation, they all commented on the need to act quickly and with compassion. When the CEOs felt they made a mistake, it was in not acting soon enough on people who no longer fit in their positions. Their lack of action had unpleasant consequences for them, for the people in question, for the team, and, in some cases, for the organization.

"I would have liked to have had the opportunity to assess the leadership and management talent of the executive team prior to becoming CEO. In addition, I believe it is important for the sitting CEO to address the talent issues prior to the transition to the new CEO. This permits the new CEO to begin with a clean slate, to establish a team that will support the transition, and to accelerate any changes in direction that the new CEO deems important."

"I learned the difficult task of dealing with an incumbent leader in the organization that I had grown up with during my career. The CFO was not what the business needed, but he had been with the organization for 32 years and had been my boss. I replaced him four years into my tenure. I should have done it two years earlier. Also, the head of HR was not well-liked by the organization or the Board."

"After a few years I made people changes and I had waited too long. We had learned nothing new and we lost good people underneath."

"I regret not acting on personnel issues more quickly. I found myself facing problematic performance and behavior in some staff. I allowed it to continue longer than I should have."

"A new CEO must determine the type of people he/she wants on the leadership team and make sure he/she has those people. At the same time, the team cannot be the 'CEO's team'—each team member must stand on his/her own virtue and compatibility with what the CEO needs. They cannot be on the 'team' because they 'agree with' the CEO or because he/she likes them. Similarly, the CEO must tolerate people he/she does not like if they bring the right skills, values, and attitude."

"The people that helped move the company to where it is today are not necessarily the people who can take it to the next milestone. To do this type of assessment in an objective manner, past loyalties and relationships must be set aside."

"The people that helped move the company to where it is today are not necessarily the people who can take it to the next milestone. To do this type of assessment in an objective manner, past loyalties and relationships must be set aside."

"Those team members who wouldn't engage, I let them go. I needed people to shout and argue with me."

"Relationships are critical to creating a solid culture but performance-based decisions must take precedent when deciding leadership positions. This can be a difficult process and emotional."

3. Leading Former Peers

Sometimes a new CEO will need to lead former peers, who perhaps also were candidates to become the CEO. When this was the case, the CEOs reported that it was important to attend to redefining their relationships with their peers.

"I spent time with my team off-site. Inclusivity was important, and I wanted to change up the dynamics of our team. I felt it was key, especially with my peers who were not selected for the CEO job. All of us went through our delicacies —but in the end, we worked well together because we committed to do so and because it was the best thing for the company."

"This contrast in the roles and the transition to CEO was difficult because I had to 'let go' of the things that I had done well in the past and that I personally enjoyed. I learned that I had to turn much of this over to others and then trust that my direct reports would do them well."

"I received a promotion ahead of my peers; they were older than me. I needed a plan of approach in dealing with them. I wish I had coaching on how to manage former peers. Suddenly, all relationships changed once I received that promotion."

"I had a strong group of colleagues when I took over. Two were competitors for the CEO job along with me, and they both stayed. (We are a promote-from-within company.)"

"I met with the two peers who were not selected the night I was named into the position. I went to dinner with them a week later. I was much more open than my predecessor was."

---

4. Leading the Team When Joining as a CEO from the Outside

Being hired in at the CEO level and joining an intact senior team, most likely with members who were also candidates but not selected for the CEO position, has its own set of unique challenges. CEOs for whom this occurred reported that it was important to build their credibility with the team while concurrently assessing the strength and weaknesses of their new colleagues.

"One thing I knew I had to do quickly, and I felt prepared to do, was to build trust and confidence in me. I had to do this with my management team and I had to do it with the other stakeholders, including the Board and with our customers."

"I joined a solid and respected senior team. My hope was that this team would stick with me. I was concerned about this because they were a talented team and also because some of the senior team members had been candidates for the CEO role. I worked hard to get to know each of the senior team members and to spend time with them. Thus far, I feel successful in that all of the top 25 people are still here. We have realigned some responsibilities, but the senior talent has continued to remain committed to the organization."

"One thing I knew I had to do quickly, and I felt prepared to do, was to build trust and confidence in me. I had to do this with my management team and I had to do it with the other stakeholders, including the Board and with our customers."

"The senior team was very solid and provided us with a marked advantage. On the other hand, the culture tended to be very analytical, and, hence, I found that decision-making was timid. The team was used to being told what to do. It was also missing key competencies."

"One thing I have learned is that it is important to be visible, and not to just be visible but to exhibit the behaviors I expect from others. People are waiting to see what I do because what I do, not what I say, is what people believe is important. I need to model the right behaviors, and I need to demand the right behaviors. Interestingly, nobody is demanding those behaviors from me, so I have to be prepared to discipline myself to exhibit them on a continuing basis."

"Communicate. I did a lot of this. Provide reinforcement from many levels about strategy, and be very visible."

"I knew that if I was going to keep the key talent, I had to get to know them and know their strengths. For the first 90 days I decided that a significant part of my role was to look, listen, and learn. I relied on some personal values I have carried with me for some time now. These are:
• Integrity—tell people the truth
• Curiosity—continually learn about the business
• Optimism—maintain a positive outlook
• Compassion—show respect for people in what I say and what I do
• Humility—be accessible and approachable"

"Communicate. I did a lot of this. Provide reinforcement from many levels about strategy, and be very visible."

5. Aligning the Senior Team

The study participants emphasized not only the criticality of having an aligned senior team, but how much time and energy they personally invested in achieving that alignment. The CEOs spoke of aligning the leadership team around the business and business issues, and around desired behaviors and culture.

"You cannot be successful unless you have an aligned team."

"Prior to becoming CEO, the leadership team was 'vertically organized' and individual members tended to work in silos. This was the case in spite of the fact that the incentive plan was designed to promote collaboration. Once I assumed my current role, I introduced a team development initiative to encourage greater collaboration and teamwork. Our time spent on off-sites and the team development has been time well spent. There is still room to get better—but we are continuing to work on this even today."

"My biggest supporters today were my biggest opponents."

"When I became CEO, I had a solid leadership team. I had worked with them for some time and knew their strengths and weaknesses. They were well-aligned with one another, and they knew our culture well. I worked to articulate what I thought was important and what I wanted as a leadership culture, and I tried to consciously exhibit those behaviors. It was true that a few were not aligned with where I wanted our leadership culture to be, but now it is much better. There still are some variances in behavior from what I would like, but they tend to be in minor areas. We have solved many of the larger issues."

"…When I became CEO we were working in silos. I began working with the leadership team to break down the silos and make it everyone's interest to have everyone succeed, not just individual divisions; we were going to become 'one company.'"

"When I have issues with my team, I call them in to discuss it immediately."

"I watch body language. I won't tolerate passive-aggressive behavior of any kind."

"There were passive-aggressive behaviors with only partial buy-in to do what we started doing organizationally. Additionally, there were deep competence and direction gaps—and a consequence history against speaking up."

"Small groups got on board but didn't have the ability to bring others along. Trust came slowly."

"It took a long time for my team to get on board with me."

"My biggest supporters today were my biggest opponents."

"I have been personally challenged by my leadership team around the issue of being a leadership team or a team of leaders. They want to run the company as a leadership team, but most of the time we are really a team of leaders."

"I have been personally challenged by my leadership team around the issue of being a leadership team or a team of leaders. They want to run the company as a leadership team, but most of the time we are really a team of leaders."

6. Developing Leadership Talent

Many of the CEOs described the need to evaluate and enrich the leadership talent at deeper levels in the organization and about the variety of developmental experiences they provided to lower-level leaders.

"We let all of the major leaders of our businesses present to the full Board at least once a year."

> *"We let all of the major leaders of our businesses present to the full Board at least once a year."*

"It is important to have regular contact with all direct reports and spend a great deal of time with them. This is the one way the CEO and COO have to get to know 'who' they are. This includes providing them with informal, real-time feedback as well as taking the lead in initiating the formal review process."

"I would love to have people rotate across different regions. Diversity must be a huge commitment. It's the future, and we must expose people to real diversity."

"Each business head presents at a major IR meeting along with a research person at least once a year."

"At our annual meeting, every business leader presents his/her business."

"Our business heads spend time with the lobbying office, working with the government, etc. These are all things of great importance today—different from when I came up through the organization."

"We rotate people between groups so they learn each other's businesses, gain exposure, etc. It really helps with business and geographic diversity."

"I take people on business trips with me, all my direct reports and the next level down. I fill up the plane with high potentials."

"We do an outstanding job in recruiting and selecting entry-level talent and then developing them into future leaders of the company. What we have not been good at—because we did not need to be —is recruiting and assimilating senior-level talent from outside the company. We needed to begin doing this if we were going to truly adapt and broaden our strategy in regard to products and geographies. I was concerned about this because a mistake here can be very costly."

"The level of our senior talent seems to be fairly strong. We might have a few issues, and I am beginning to learn where they are. Some of these issues are at the senior team level, but I believe they exist in even greater numbers at the mid-management level. This was not so much a surprise as it was simply an unknown at the time. The company has not had a systematic leadership assessment and development program, and implementing one will be one of my first priorities. As an early step, I brought in some people I have worked with in the past and whose strengths are important to me and to our company."

"Make sure CEO successor candidates have had a variety of experiences so you've seen them in different circumstances. If you put people in jobs that you know they can do well, then why bother putting them in it? Where is the growth for them or the organization in that assignment, then? People need to be given the chance to show the company what they can do. That begins with really spending time on getting them the right assignments."

"I would look for someone who has made tough decisions and faced crises; someone who has taken a few hard licks—like a quarterback who has been sacked a few times. When you have been sacked you learn to call plays differently."

Recommendations

First, recognize that people are critical to any success you might achieve as CEO. In this job, perhaps more than any other job, you will depend on your senior team and the people below them to carry out the company's vision, make effective decisions, and drive the right actions in the organization. While you might be ultimately responsible for the company's most strategic decisions, you will never have all of the information you need to make them nor the time needed to successfully implement them by yourself. This is where a talented and aligned senior team is critical to your success.

When you become CEO, people will expect you to articulate what you stand for as early as day one—your values about people, what you stand for as a leader, your perspective on the importance of operating as a team. In fact, your values about people are likely to play into whether or not you are selected for the job of CEO in the first place. People will interpret your words and actions in ways that will affect their behavior for a long time to come.

Be prepared. Define your values about people and how you lead people. Define how you expect your senior team to operate. Be ready to talk with others about your values, and, of course, remember that actions speak louder than words. Ensure that your behavior is consistent with your values when it comes to making decisions that affect people—whether they impact one person or the entire organization.

Here are specific recommendations that emerged from the study findings:

Selecting/Evaluating the Senior Team

- As a new CEO, one of your first jobs will be to assess your senior team. Most likely, you will find yourself making difficult decisions about whether some people are still a fit for the team. People will anticipate that you will make changes to your senior team. How you handle these changes will define you for years to come. Ideally, each person who ultimately leaves the organization will leave with only good things to say about you and about the company—that they were treated fairly and with respect. It is up to you to make sure that happens.

- Ensure that the competencies, values, and behaviors you want people on the senior team to have and to exhibit are described in writing.

- Ensure that there is a tool to informally but systematically evaluate each of the senior team members.

- Gather as much information as you can about individual team members and the functioning of the team as a whole from your predecessor and from other sources, including reviewing their performance records. Schedule dedicated time with your predecessor to review the team and team members. If possible, ask your predecessor to address lingering performance issues prior to departing from that position.

- Assess people objectively. Evaluate each member of the team with regard to the competencies and behaviors you would like to see exhibited, and determine the extent to which each person's behavior is compatible with the vision and values of the company going forward. Where there are gaps, determine the extent to which you believe they can close those gaps.

- If you bring in senior talent from the outside, make sure you set them up for success. Your senior team, then the rest of the organization, needs to understand why you are bringing in external talent rather than filling the position from inside. This is an easier task if you are hiring for a skill set that was not a priority in the organization previously (e.g., you are hiring for the company's first-ever Chief Learning Officer). It is more difficult if you are upgrading talent because the company does not have people who are ready for the role but who might expect to be considered for it.

Acting on Talent Gaps or Issues

- The main message from the CEOs in the study was to not wait too long to address talent issues. Articulate your new expectations, and give everyone a chance to perform. Make sure you are regularly talking with them about how it's working so there are no surprises.

- If there are competency gaps on your team that can be filled right away, do so. For example, if the team is lacking a needed strategic communications person or Chief Information Officer, move quickly to find the right person.

- If there are people who are not a fit for your new team, act compassionately to help them move on. Remember, this is a stressful time for them, too. They are coping with having a new leader with new priorities and perhaps different values from their previous boss. Your job is to help them understand what you expect and give them the opportunity to perform, if they choose to. At the end of the day, if you do part ways, your goal should be to do so on good terms.

Leading Former Peers

- It is not always easy to navigate the waters when it comes to leading former peers. You will need to redefine your relationship with each individual, and, in some cases, you will need to let go of aspects of your past. Take concrete steps such as asking for a meeting with them, inviting them to dinner to talk openly about the relationship or past, or go to the cities in which they live to talk with them about what you will need from them going forward.

- If one or more of your peers was also a candidate for the CEO role, recognize that they will probably be in the middle of deciding whether or not they will choose to stay with the company. If it is the right thing for them to stay with the company, recognize the importance of your personal involvement in convincing them to stay on board as a fully contributing member of the senior team. Go out of your way to tell them privately and demonstrate publicly that you value their talents and contributions—make your support for them undeniable.

- Clear out the past and set new agreements for the future. Do this soon to show you are not afraid to address issues now, even if you have avoided them in the past. Do something symbolic to show the game has changed.

Leading the Team When Joining as CEO from the Outside

- Learn as much as you can about each senior team member before you come on board. If possible, talk to your predecessor, your Board, and/or any trusted advisors about the individuals on your team. You want to understand their strengths and weaknesses across a number of dimensions: their functional expertise, their ability to work in a team, their ability to lead others, their credibility in the organization, etc. Take note of what you hear from several people about your team members that is consistent, and what you hear that's inconsistent. This will help you identify areas you want to probe more deeply when you come on board.

> *"At a minimum, your role in leadership development is to be an active steward of the company's succession planning process..."*

- When you come on board, schedule individual conversations with each of your senior team members. Meet with them at their locations. While you might have learned about them, or perhaps even met some of them during the selection process, neither of you are yet ready to jump into working with each other. This discussion should be about getting to know each other—your values, your goals, and your hopes for your relationship and the organization. Agree on the next steps you will take to deepen your working relationship. In subsequent conversations, you will quickly turn to topics related to business goals, strategies, metrics, etc.

- Consider asking a neutral—perhaps external—facilitator to conduct a "new leader assimilation" for you and your new team. In this forum, the facilitator works individually with the team and with the CEO to draw out mutual expectations and to define critical behaviors. Then the facilitator works with the CEO and team together to discuss those expectations and make agreements as to how they will operate.

- Another way to get to know your senior team better is by talking with people who report up to them. Conversations with your senior team's direct reports can be sensitive, but they can also be a good way for you to introduce yourself to the organization and to round out your assessment of your leadership team members and of the culture. Make sure your senior leadership team is involved in helping you prepare for and communicate about the direct report meetings so that you have their buy-in and so the rest of the organization sees it. Share with your senior team what you will and won't do during the direct report sessions and how you will debrief with them.

> *"The fastest path to getting the behaviors you want from your senior team is to name and praise them when you see those behaviors."*

Aligning the Senior Team

- Define how you would like the senior team to operate. Do you want them to operate as a leadership team, or a team of leaders? How often do you want the team to meet? How will you run your leadership team meetings? What decisions does that group need to make? What performances do they need to steward? What key metrics will keep them aligned and supportive of one another's business success?

- The fastest path to getting the behaviors you want from your senior team is to name and praise them when you see those behaviors. People will quickly learn what you value. While your senior team is most likely composed of bright and previously successful executives, they will not know right away, how to interpret your leadership words and actions—and you need to help them know what you expect and desire from them—or they will be left to their own devices to figure that out. This can be costly in many dimensions—mainly in terms of their modeling behaviors that are incompatible with what you want and expect of others.

- In the same vein, be clear about what is unacceptable to you —behaviors that you feel undermine the team, the culture, the business. If you see those behaviors, call them quickly and firmly. If you don't, not only will you make it more difficult to align your senior team, you will set the stage to erode performance as well as your own credibility.

- Review how the organization is structured and how metrics are used to evaluate performance (and to award individual compensation). Determine if there are any major misalignments in how you expect your team to operate with how their performance is measured, evaluated, and rewarded. Recognize that you will probably never achieve perfection, but major misalignments should be corrected. In some cases, you might need help from your senior HR person or possibly an external consultant to better align these areas.

- Be conscious of with whom you spend your time. For the new CEO, whether an internal selection or an external selection, it can be easy to default to those members of the senior team with whom you are most comfortable. Other team members will be aware of how you allocate your time, and this can telegraph an unintended message.

- Consciously exhibit the behaviors you want to see in others. People will be watching the new CEO, and what the new CEO does is far more important than what he/she says.

Developing Leadership Talent

- As CEO, you will be concerned with the leadership bench strength in your organization because it represents the company's continuity and longevity. In some cases, you will become frustrated with the lack of concern your senior team and others have about this topic. It is your role to set the tone for the importance of developing leaders. It is also your role to set the example for how leaders will be developed within the company.

- One of your first steps in developing leadership talent will be to begin planning for the development of your successor.

- At a minimum, your role in leadership development is to be an active steward of the company's succession planning process and an active performance coach for your senior team members.

- Beyond the minimum, you will have many choices to make about how to focus the organization's attention and resources on leadership development, and, of course, your senior HR person should have a clear and compelling point of view on this topic.

- As many of the study participants identified, one additional way the CEO can visibly demonstrate a personal interest in developing leaders is to provide high-potential leaders with access to people and experiences they might not otherwise get. This could be in the form of presenting to the Board, traveling with the CEO on some occasions, participating in senior business reviews, etc.

TEN

WORKING WITH YOUR BOARD OF DIRECTORS

The Board of Directors is a primary stakeholder group for the CEO. As such, the study participants reported spending significant time and energy preparing for and interacting with the Board. If the CEO's relationship with the Board and its individual members is strong, time and effectiveness can be greatly enhanced. If the relationship is strained or difficult, it will create challenges and impediments for the CEO, and likely add to the workloads on both sides without adding a commensurate amount of value.

The CEOs also emphasized that their roles include working with the Board and its collective dynamics, but also developing working relationships with each individual Board member. Both the collective Board relationship and the unique individual member relationships are integral to effective governance.

"The CEO must spend a great deal of time in managing the Board and working with members individually."

STUDY HIGHLIGHTS

By the time they were named CEO, nearly all of the study participants had served on one or more Boards, often non-profit Boards of various groups. All had some exposure to the Boards they would be leading, primarily as presenters or guests in key meetings. They identified experiences on other Boards and knowledge of how Boards work, in general, as important to their preparedness for their role as CEO. In the few cases that a new CEO did not have Board experience, he/she lamented that it was a noticeable gap in his/her preparation.

"I would say I wasn't adequately prepared to work with the Board. I had not participated on the Board and was not on any outside Boards."

> *"I had almost no exposure to the Board prior to becoming CEO. When I started I had to learn this quickly. I had been to only three BOD meetings prior to selection."*

When the CEOs spoke about what they learned as they began to work with their Boards once in the CEO role, they commented on a handful of topics, including:

- The need to develop good relationships with Board members and the influence of those relationships on the Board's working dynamics.
- The dynamics of assuming the CEO role if his/her predecessor is the Chairman (and previous CEO).
- The need to select one or more Board members during their tenure.
- The role of the Board in planning for the CEO's succession.

The CEOs' experiences and comments are detailed in the following section, in these categories:

1. Prior exposure and experiences working with the CEO's Board
2. Developing personal relationships with Board members
3. Dynamics with the Board and impact on CEO/Board effectiveness
4. Impact on CEOs of Board members' increased accountability
5. Dynamics of Chairman and CEO roles and succession of CEO to Chairman
6. Selecting Board members
7. Board's involvement in CEO succession

Detailed Findings

What follows are the CEO's descriptions of the dynamics they encountered in selecting and working with their Boards and their learnings about what it takes to work effectively with their Boards to govern their organizations.

1. Prior Exposure and Experience Working with the CEO's Board

As described earlier, the CEOs who did have more experience working with their Boards reported it to be helpful in getting to know the individual Board members and in learning to work with the Board.

"I sat on the Board for one year, which was not enough time to assess the strengths/needs of outside Board members. I wished I could have established an independent relationship with outside Board members. This was disallowed by my predecessor."

"The BOD, which for us is an internal BOD, does not present a major issue for me. My exposure to the BOD prior to becoming CEO was intentionally limited in order to not telegraph my candidacy for becoming the CEO. I did note that there are members of the BOD who are generally supportive of my leadership and offer their expertise in addressing issues, and there are those who are more problematic and difficult to work with."

> "… time with the Board was invaluable in providing me insights on how our Board worked and the personalities of the various Board members…"

"Prior to becoming CEO, I had served on the Board for two years. This time with the Board was invaluable in providing me insights on how our Board worked and the personalities of the various Board members, and it allowed me to become comfortable working with them. More importantly, it led to greater mutual trust, which, in turn, has allowed us to become candid and direct with one another. I have been impressed that our Board has consistently worked with the best interests of the company in mind."

"Because I had spent time with the Board, I felt well-prepared to assume a leadership role with them."

"Join an outside Board. Be selective about which one you choose to be sure it is something that is interesting to you and will be helpful to you or the company in some way. It is an excellent way to continue your own learning, which is so important."

2. Developing Personal Relationships with Board Members

In addition to having exposure and the opportunity to work with the Board, the study participants found it necessary to invest in developing personal relationships with Board members. The participating CEOs described what they did—and what they wish they had done—in getting to know their Board members in order to develop effective working relationships.

"I spend at least 25% of my time managing these relationships."

"Although I had interacted with the Board as COO, when I assumed the role of CEO, their expectations of me changed, as did the nature of my relationship with them. I also found that I had to work not only with the Board as an entity but with individual members of the Board, each of whom has a unique set of expectations and objectives. I found that I had to manage relationships and conflicts among the Board members and work to resolve rifts when they began to appear."

"For the first six to nine months I was in the CEO job, my wife and I went to the home city of each Director and had one-on-one meetings with them. In some cases, we spent the weekends with them. There were 13 of them and it was important for me to cement relationships with each of them. We are very transparent here—and I wanted to model that, even in my early weeks and months."

"Today we have a Board that is 50% new since the merger. I do one-on-ones with them every other year to engender a positive, personal relationship with each of them."

"On my Board, I have great friendships, great advisorship; it's a great Board."

"Having a well-functioning Board is key. Be sure to have structured and unstructured time with your Board in advance of becoming CEO. Find a way to learn how Boards operate, and ask questions of your CEO to learn more about your own Board (including what happens when you are out of the room)."

"For the first six to nine months I was in the CEO job, my wife and I went to the home city of each Director and had one-on-one meetings with them. In some cases, we spent the weekends with them...."

"I conducted an exhaustive due diligence on the Board of Directors when I was being recruited for the CEO job. I completed a Google™ search on each person to get as much data as I could. I went to meet each of them in the cities in which they live. I asked them about their expectations. I tried to focus on four buckets: Strategy/planning, succession and development, metrics, and culture. On my second trip to meet with them in the cities in which they lived, I took the Board of Directors and their spouses to dinner. These meetings prepared me for legacy with the Board. I am closest to Directors I met first through the search process—and the Committee Chairs and Lead Director."

3. Dynamics with the Board and Impact on CEO/Board Effectiveness

The CEO's relationship with the Board is important to his/her effectiveness as chief executive and satisfaction with the job. The CEOs reported that their relationships are both with individual directors as well as the collective Board, and that both require significant time and energy.

> *"As CEO, my relationship with the Board has changed significantly. Rather than reporting to the Board on operating results during scheduled meetings, the Board, collectively, and each member, individually, require a significant portion of my time between meetings. Rather than reporting to the Board, I now report to the Board plus each individual member of the Board."*

> *"I was managing the expectations of ten people. They are your boss, but you have to help teach them and bring them along."*

When the CEO and Board establish and continuously improve upon a mutually effective relationship, the CEOs reported feeling well supported. They see their jobs as maintaining transparency in and with their Boards and ensuring that their Boards have the information needed to fulfill their governance roles.

> *"I was well prepared for the amount of time required for communicating to various stakeholders, including the Board and the public. There has been a long history of good communications between executive management and the Board."*

> *"We have a good Board. They are very engaged and add a great deal of value. Furthermore, I have a good working relationship with them."*

> *"I see the Board is there to help me and to help the company."*

"I communicate much more to the Board than my predecessor did, and the Board loves it."

"I see the Board as my kitchen cabinet."

"I needed to become more transparent with the Board, and this is still developing. We continue to learn to try different things. I would describe this as an ongoing evolution."

"You have to be able to tell your Board what is not going well, such as governance issues, risk assessment. The Board must feel I am being honest and transparent with them, and working on areas where we have vulnerabilities."

When the relationship between the CEO and the Board is more contentious, CEOs reported stressful interactions—in some cases, adversarial interactions.

"The issues with the Board of Directors, while I was aware of it as an abstract problem, became more stressful when it was my issue. I had a hard time getting people to be courageous. For four years, I didn't make much progress. It was a contentious relationship with the Board of Directors. Then we had a bad quarter, and it got bad right away. This is when we had different points of view of what leadership should do."

"The current challenge with the Board is the communication strategy—getting them to buy into the strategy for the company."

"I refused to be intimidated by the Board."

A handful of CEOs reported that one factor in a difficult working relationship with the Board is the degree to which the Board members are aligned with each other and working effectively. If the directors have different points of view and are not communicating effectively with each other, the CEO must spend more time with them individually and collectively to reach resolution.

"One thing that would have helped me would have been to know how cohesive and aligned the Board was and to what extent they were truly involved in running the business. I spent a significant amount of time with them discussing the company's future and their vision for the company, but it wasn't clear that they held a common view. They did not seem to be as engaged in the company as other Boards with whom I have worked. As a result, it was also difficult for me to truly evaluate the strengths and weaknesses of the Board collectively, as well as individual Board members."

> *"You have to be able to tell your Board what is not going well..."*

"This Board had consultants for everything when I joined the company. They had outside attorneys. Everyone went to everyone's meetings but didn't communicate well with one another."

4. Impact on CEOs of Board Members' Increased Accountability

In part, recent trends in corporate governance expectations have been the cause of CEOs and Boards redefining their working relationships.

"The workings of the BOD have changed a lot in the past two to four years—in the post-Enron environment. Things like audit, comp, and governance have very demanding responsibilities with many people to answer to."

"The Board and I had to face dramatic changes in the regulatory environment such as Sarbanes-Oxley. This meant we had to address issues of governance, including the role of the Board and the inherent liabilities that were now made explicit."

"The Board and I had to face dramatic changes in the regulatory environment such as Sarbanes-Oxley. This meant we had to address issues of governance, including the role of the Board and the inherent liabilities that were now made explicit."

"At the time I became CEO, significant changes in corporate governance began to occur in American industry. These changes, in turn, required significant changes in our governance, and architecting and ensuring compliance with these changes has taken a great deal of mine and the Board's time. As a result, I have strengthened our governance processes and the capabilities of the people involved. It has required a lot of work—restructuring, new hires, and has distracted the BOD at times that were not helpful."

5. Dynamics of Chairman and CEO Roles and Succession of CEO to Chairman

A handful of the study's participants commented on the dynamics of becoming CEO when their predecessor remained as Chairman. There was not a clear consensus as to whether the CEOs supported the separation of the Chairman and CEO roles. A couple of CEOs were quite firm in their assertion that the outgoing CEO should not serve in the Chairman role. Others felt that an overlap with the former CEO as the Chairman, for a few months or for up to a year, could be helpful if the Chairman was able to stay in his/her (new) swim lane and let the (new) CEO do his/her job without interference.

"It's hard to be all three roles (Chairman, CEO, President) if you believe in the importance of all three roles."

"The current trend in corporate governance appears to have led many companies to separate the role of the Chairman from the role of the CEO. This separation tends to dilute the power that is embodied in the consolidated role and potentially can create redundancy, confusion, and conflict in the separated roles. One advantage of separating the roles is that it reduces potential distractions created by Board responsibilities for the CEO."

"It is a disservice to the company and to the incoming CEO to have the Chairman stay on without a clear role definition. The transition needs to be clear and crisp. No one talks about what's best for the company; they always talk about what's best for so-and-so… or how so-and-so will handle the transition. It would be so much better and simpler if we simply did what was best for the company!"

"I believe that the retiring CEO should not become Chairman. The new CEO is inheriting the structure and culture created by the prior CEO and may find it necessary to significantly alter the organization."

"He was Executive Chairman for six months, and non-Executive Chairman for one year. That was extremely helpful for me as I was not, then, overlapping with him for BOD leadership."

6. Selecting Board Members

A few of the CEOs in the study stated that they needed to—or anticipated needing to—select new Board members during their tenure. They see this as an important opportunity to provide the company with governance aligned with its current and future needs. In some cases, selecting Board members can be complicated by the CEO's relationship with his or her predecessor, if the predecessor is serving as the company's Chairman. If the relationship is strained, then selecting a new Board member can become a point of contention.

"Over the past six years, one-half of our BOD has turned over due to retirements, etc., and that has allowed me to recruit folks that match up well with our current/future needs."

"Over the past six years, one-half of our BOD has turned over due to retirements, etc., and that has allowed me to recruit folks that match up well with our current/future needs."

"When I stepped in as CEO, he was the Chairman of the Board. It was his Board. Any change I introduced was reflected as criticism of him."

"I was a 'friend of his Board of Directors.' On day 20, it was 'time to pick a few BOD members.' He was Chairman and did most of the talking. Even the new Board members joined because of him. It wasn't until the third Board member that I got my choice. He was a good friend of the Chairman's—they vacationed together. At the time of the LBO, the first time, I could really alter the Board members. I cleaned house; I could not have done that with the Chairman here."

7. Board's Involvement in CEO Succession

When it comes to planning for their succession, the CEOs in the study drew from their own experiences in recommending the nature of the Board's participation in selecting a successor and how to have a successful start with the Board.

"I will set up places now where people who have functional responsibility are visible and have access to the Board."

"I have tried to increase the team's exposure to the Board of Directors directly, but when a confrontation occurs, the Board of Directors shuts the door."

"The Board has to be aligned with the process of selecting the CEO and with bringing the new CEO into the Board. They have to be comfortable with the new CEO."

"It will be important to provide opportunities for my successor to work with the Board members collectively and individually in order to establish personal connections and to allow the incoming CEO to make his/her own assessments of the Board's strengths and weaknesses."

"I have tried to increase the team's exposure to the Board of Directors directly, but when a confrontation occurs, the Board of Directors shuts the door."

"The more exposure the Board has to potential succession candidates for the CEO role, the more Board support there will be for a candidate once selected."

"Whoever is chosen to be the successor, if the person is internal, I would encourage the Board to probe if the person has courage and challenge whether the internal candidates believe in the need for change at the highest levels of the organization. The person needs to have skills and vision to do this."

RECOMMENDATIONS

Prepare yourself to devote the time and energy required to work effectively with the Board to govern the company. The study participants said they spent up to 25% of their time working with the Board individually and collectively to ensure an effective working relationship.

While the CEO might officially report to the Board, or specifically to the Chairman (if the CEO and Chairman positions are separate), the importance of individual working relationships with the Board members cannot be discounted. It is also important that the CEO create opportunities for his/her direct reports to develop relationships with the Board. This comes with face-to-face interaction, not only in formal presentations, but also through dialogues on selected topics and in casual conversation.

Take time to think about—and record—the type of working relationship you would like to have with the Board and with each individual member, and what will be required to achieve it. What do you expect of your Board? Some of the factors that will influence your working relationship will include:

Your Current Working Relationships with Individuals on the Board

- Prepare a "plan" for your relationship with the Board and for each member of the Board.

- Schedule time to meet with each Board member in his/her home city. Get to know them as individuals and listen to their perspective on the company, their expectations for you/your success, and how they can best be a resource to you and, therefore, to the company's success.

Your Working Relationship with the Chairman, Particularly if He/She Is Your Predecessor as CEO

- It will be important for you and the Chairman to meet privately to discuss how you will handle the changes in your roles as well as your Board responsibilities. This might be more or less difficult depending on the circumstances surrounding both of your role transitions. Regardless, you both have a responsibility to do all you can to work well together on the Board for the good of the company.

- Some specific areas of conversation include how you will coordinate communication with the directors, preparation for Board meetings, management of the Board during meetings, selection of new Board members (if there are current or anticipated openings on the Board), desired changes to committee structure or membership, current items pending before the Board, and so on.

- Pay particular attention to staying in sync with the Chairman prior to and following each Board meeting. While the two of you might not see eye-to-eye on every issue, it will be important to demonstrate that you are working together to ensure that the Board operates smoothly and provides the governance the company needs.

Your Working Relationship with the Board

- What is the nature of your relationship? Do you see your Board as a group of people who are there to help you and the company, or do you feel you need to be guarded in what you share with them and how you involve them in decision making?

- What expectations does the Board have of you? If you are not clear on how they expect you to interact with them, it will be important to have that conversation. Consider retaining a Board consultant to facilitate this conversation, not only because it removes the burden for leading the conversation from you or one of the directors, but also because a consultant will have expertise to offer and observations you might find helpful.

- Prior to Board meetings, contact each Board member and discuss the agenda topics.

- Debrief each Board member soon after the Board meeting is finished.

The Extent to Which the Directors Communicate and Work Well with Each Other

- Are the directors living up to your expectations? Do they come to meetings prepared? Have they performed their necessary committee work? Are they communicating openly and thoroughly with one another? Are any of them complaining about each other to you privately? Are any of them trying to give you direction without consulting the rest of the Board?

- If the Board is working well, be sure to share what you think is working, and express your appreciation. If the Board is not working well, you will need a plan to confront the issues. You might need to employ the assistance of the Chairman, one or more directors, or a Board consultant to do so.

The Extent to Which You and the Directors Have a Cohesive Point of View About Major Decisions Impacting the Company's Governance and Shareholder Value

- One of the benefits of a Board is the wealth of experience they bring to the table. This means that they will not always agree with each other or with you, and this is often a good thing because it forces rich conversation about the pros and cons associated with significant decisions. However, there comes a point at which a Board must come to a shared point of view about major decisions with significant governance and shareholder consequences; otherwise you, the CEO, will be stuck between a rock and a hard place.

- Many times the Board will be able to come to a shared point of view, provided they have sufficient data and adequate time for dialogue about the issue at hand. If you find yourself in a situation with repeated or irreconcilable differences, it is time to look at whether you are the right person for the CEO job and/or whether one or more directors is still the right fit for the Board.

Your Vision for Future Board Members

- You will likely have turnover at the Board level during your time at the helm. Think about the profile of Board members you would like to recruit. What skill sets would complement those that already exist?

- As you are being interviewed for the job of CEO or during your first 100 days in the position, it will be important to assess each of these factors and develop an action plan for improving the areas that will impede your effectiveness with the Board. Your action plan might involve:

  - *Individual Conversation(s) with Individual Directors and/or the Chairman* — you most certainly need to invest one-on-one time with each director and the Chairman, in part to begin to develop, or to enhance, an existing personal relationship and to begin to share expectations and perhaps work through pre-existing issues.

  - *A Board Meeting Focused on Clarifying Roles, Responsibilities, and Expectations* — you will need to define or influence more aspects of how the Board operates, the frequency with which you communicate with members, the degree of transparency into the business you give them, etc. Don't leave these defining aspects of your relationship with the Board to chance. Decide how you want things to operate, and make it happen.

ELEVEN

BEING CEO TO THE OUTSIDE WORLD

I nherent in the position, the CEO is the name, face, and voice of the company to the outside world and to all external stakeholders, including:

- Regulators
- Analysts and investors
- Press
- Community
- Heads of state

"We believe that much of what happens in the executive office is 'secret,' but in truth, employees and even external audiences know what is occurring..."

The participating CEOs understood the obligation inherent in their role to meet the outside world's need to have one person's name, face, and voice representing the company. What the CEO says and does on significant occasions, is synonymous with the company, and as the incumbent is judged, so is the company judged. As the embodiment of their companies, the CEOs commented that it is critical to be honest and transparent when they represent their companies to the outside world.

"We believe that much of what happens in the executive office is 'secret,' but in truth, employees and even external audiences know what is occurring. It is better to be transparent with this information than to continue to believe it is hidden."

On the other hand, they commented that communications with the outside world must be precise in order to avoid misunderstandings and misinterpretation. Communicating with the outside world was a responsibility that many CEOs reported was something they were less well prepared for than other parts of the job.

"Communications must be precise. Things will get amplified. There is a whole host of preparation that is essential."

The demands from external stakeholders for time and information combined with a deep feeling of accountability for communicating clearly and accurately—and in a way that is not likely to be misinterpreted—places enormous demands on CEOs.

STUDY HIGHLIGHTS

The CEO study participants consistently identified dealing with external stakeholders as an important part of their job.

"There are huge investor relations challenges and pressures that continue to intensify coming at us from the external environment. A company like ours can't NOT get involved. We must."

"The world dynamics have changed so much. The role of CEO of a global company demands a lot of a global CEO."

"I must be prepared to present a proper and professional public image as an individual and as the representative of the company, and to meet with heads of state and the new media."

In many cases, being the CEO to the outside world is a part of the job the study participants were not fully prepared to take on. Within the last several years, in particular, the study participants consistently said that expectations have changed. Sarbanes-Oxley (SOX) legislation, globalization, and other demands have intensified the need for the CEO to be personally involved and well-versed on a myriad of issues that external stakeholders are concerned about.

"I was not as well prepared for being the CEO to the outside world, and I didn't really need to be better prepared the way you do now. I had formal training on all three of these areas—but the requirements of these things are so different from when I first came into this role."

"I was well prepared for the internal responsibilities. I was less well prepared for the external responsibilities."

In some cases, the CEOs reported being caught off guard by the adversarial stance that external stakeholders often take. One CEO characterized this adversarial stance in this way:

"(The external stakeholders think that) institutions are not to be trusted. CEOs embody the notion of the institution."

Nor did the CEOs anticipate the toll the public scrutiny would take on themselves and their families.

"It's a cold, tough community that can have a thankless relationship."

"One significant challenge has been working with various regulatory agencies and the orientation of members of those agencies. In some ways, I had a naïve view that if we communicated with the agencies and told them what we were doing, and I answered their questions candidly, we would move forward together. What I discovered is that they are adversarial by nature. They operate with a mindset that they seek to find something to accuse you of. It took me awhile to realize this and know how to handle this."

"I was surprised at how brutal the analyst community and the press are. They were all negative."

"I didn't realize the public scrutiny or how people would criticize me and my family. It takes a toll professionally and personally."

"I didn't realize how public my life as a CEO would be; it was much more than I imagined—from my compensation to the business news coverage."

"I must continually be mindful of what I say and how I say it. It is so easy to say things in a way that leads to misinterpretation or over-interpretation by any of my constituencies. It just seems to be human nature to read more into my comments and even in my inflections than was intended."

"I didn't realize how public my life as a CEO would be; it was much more than I imagined—from my compensation to the business news coverage."

"I am always 'on.' I am on every day with employees, with Congress, and with customers, and it is tiring. Sometimes I look at my schedule and I know that I must show up all the time and be engaging. Not being 'on' impacts the group negatively, and that is unintentional. Sometimes, I don't think it's even a reasonable expectation."

The CEOs' experiences and comments are detailed in the following section, in these categories:

1. **Recommended preparation for fulfilling the CEO's external role**

2. **What it's like to deal with external stakeholders, by audience (regulators, analysts and investors, press, community, heads of state)**

Detailed Findings

1. Recommended Preparation for Fulfilling the CEO's External Role

Many of the CEOs in the study felt less prepared to play the role of CEO to the outside world than they did for handling many of the other CEO responsibilities. In some cases, they had been exposed to some subsets of external stakeholders and felt equipped to interact with them. However, many reported learning how to interact with the external community, in part, through their mistakes.

"Presenting information to analysts and discussing the implications of that information is an area I believe is not formally nor sufficiently addressed in preparing CEO candidates. The whole practice of taking quarterly earnings to analysts, and how to prepare for these conversations, is really important to focus on, and I don't think succession management does a great job of teaching this."

"Presenting information to analysts and discussing the implications of that information is an area I believe is not formally nor sufficiently addressed in preparing CEO candidates..."

"I was surprised as to the extent of external obligations for the CEO. I had a lot of learnings around prioritization, necessity of time requirement, and obligations that simply came with the job. It would not have been possible to be fully prepared for many of these activities in that they are 'open' only to the sitting CEO."

"I suggest formal training to prepare for the investor relations role of today."

"I didn't know the banking or investor banking world, and it was a world I had to interact a lot with."

"Get experience where you are required to communicate as the sole communicator for your company."

"For the five years before becoming CEO, I had worked with the analysts, so I have had no problems continuing to work with them."

"I began doing investment relation road shows four to five years before becoming CEO. This was a great risk by my CEO. This part of the transition went extremely well. My boss was right not to do this when it would be OK to make mistakes. The way you speak to the investment community is completely different from how you communicate with anyone else."

"In my previous roles, I had spent a great deal of time dealing with the press and the media and felt quite comfortable continuing to work with them."

"The investor community was new to me. I had to learn quickly how to talk to investors and analysts. I was a bit surprised by how much depth I had to go into with them."

2. What It's Like to Deal with External Stakeholders, by Audience

Regulators

SOX and other financial reporting requirements are particularly daunting for CEOs.

"The CEO must be highly knowledgeable of regulatory and compliance issues. These can be daunting to a new CEO."

"The year that SOX was implemented, I was very surprised by the amount of time and energy the implementation took out of the organization. For example, the manual work required was immense."

"One area where I am continually exasperated is the frequent and seemingly unending changes in regulatory issues around the world and changes in accounting guidelines."

Analysts and Investors

Communicating with analysts and investors was mentioned repeatedly as a particularly important, and sometimes difficult, part of the CEO's job. Many CEOs shared that they and their organizations carefully plan for and debrief each and every call to continually improve their performance.

"We read transcripts from investor calls to determine what we want to communicate and determine what is private and what is public information, and we also read transcripts and listen to calls from our competitors."

"I read every transcript from my analysts' presentation so I can learn from it and do better the next time."

"The CEO must work at maintaining the relationships with the market. They cannot be placated, and the CEO must be truthful with them. Take advantage of the media as a vehicle to deliver your messages."

"Agree on the approach the company takes with the investors. We take a thoughtful and disciplined approach to investors and do not provide more information than absolutely necessary. We spend significant time preparing our communications to analysts. Our CFO and SVP of our largest BU have a significant amount of face time with investors. We also spend a significant amount of time preparing for the calls together. I believe it's important for the CFO and SVP to have an understanding of the investors and for the investors to gain confidence in people other than me."

"We have internal rules, such as no piling on and letting others handle questions in their area of expertise during the analysts' presentations."

"An early mistake that I made was delegating too much responsibility to others for managing the company's relationships with the investment community. In retrospect, I should have devoted more time and attention to these relationships and established a more effective presence with shareholders. In addition, I could have made better use of the media in conveying the messages I wanted to communicate."

Press

The CEO is a very public figure, and the press tends to personalize both the good and the bad and attribute it to the CEO.

"The media writes about me endlessly. The reporters wrote articles for three months straight after I was named CEO. Finally, there was a great editorial in the press that simply said, 'Leave the new CEO alone. Let her do her job. She earned it.'"

"I chafe when the company is criticized because I know the people, our employees, get criticized. I feel less badly if it's about me than I do if it's about the company—mainly because of what our people experience."

"I didn't realize how public my life as a CEO would be. It was much more than I imagined—from my compensation to the business news coverage."

"The press tends to personalize every event and accomplishment. Our company's culture is all about 'we' and teamwork... which is what I would say to them... but inevitably in print, it would come out as 'I.' They attribute everything the company does to the CEO. It seems they want the CEO to appear 'interesting.' I should mention that they attribute everything to the CEO, whether it is good or bad."

"The CEO title has greater impact in some ways on the spouse and family than it does on the incumbent. My wife and kids read about me in the press, some of it flattering and some of it not—and some of it is factual and some of it is simply not true. They even write about my wife."

Community

The CEO is sought out by the community to support any number of causes.

"Community involvement is important for the image of the company, but is equally important for the employees in that such involvement 'validates' their decision to work for the company and how they are perceived by family and friends."

Heads of State

"Heads of State will only meet with one person: the CEO. The family and spouse, especially, need to buy into all of this and what the commitment of being CEO really entails, and be ready to support and participate fully in the process."

Recommendations

Recognizing the importance of preparing yourself for the role of being CEO to the outside world, you can best prepare yourself by learning from others currently in that role and by cultivating your own public persona before you become CEO.

Observe how your current CEO interacts with the outside world

- If possible, observe him or her firsthand — for example, attend meetings with regulators or attend a preparatory or debrief session for an analyst call. If you cannot, you can attend analyst calls and observe the CEO's words and performance. Or you can read the press about your company and the CEO and contemplate how the press interpreted your CEO's message, based on your own knowledge. Capture, in writing, what you liked and did not like about your CEO's performance in these situations. Spend time contemplating or discussing with your coach how you might approach that situation differently.

Read the detailed transcripts from investor and analyst calls from other companies in your industry and outside your industry

- Many of these are available online. Again, answer questions about what you felt they did well and what they did not do as well. Develop your own lists of do's and don'ts for those types of interactions.

Spend time with your head of investor relations

- Learn from him/her what the current dynamics are for your company and the shareholder analyst community. Schedule regular briefings with him/her to continue intensifying your own learnings here. Invite his/her input as to what the company is doing well and concerns/challenges they see. Demonstrate your openness to coaching, guidance, and feedback from them. Convey your expectation for their conveying "early warning signs" to you, versus waiting for you to ask.

Become fluent with Sarbanes-Oxley, in particular

- Understand what requirements it places on the CEO, CFO, and other officers. Talk with peer CEOs on how they have modified their leadership and organizational processes, and what they learned in the process.

Continue to cultivate your public persona

- As CEO, people will be interested in who you are and what you stand for.

  - *Be selective* about what charitable opportunities you become involved in. Make sure they are consistent with your values and also with the public image of your company. Just as importantly, recognize the limits on your availability, especially early on.

  - *Explore external sources for media training* if you feel you have a developmental need in that area.

  - *Work with an executive coach* to help you prepare your 100-day plan and prepare for some of the important, early conversations with the various stakeholder groups.

Talk with your family

- Make sure they are ready to deal with you being in the public eye —in particular, being criticized publicly.

Develop a thick skin

- First, recognize that many external stakeholders are not looking to be friendly; in fact, their jobs are to question and challenge you. Sometimes it can become adversarial. Remain respectful and professional. Second, try to separate your emotions and be objective about your performance with external stakeholders. You will learn from every interaction, and you can use that learning to improve your performance next time. As one of the CEOs in the study said:

"It was important for me to understand my reactions to publicly delivered criticism and to separate myself from these comments. I needed to continue to address business and organizational issues in an objective and dispassionate manner. I became more immune to the criticism than I thought I would, and I was able to maintain my equanimity during some very difficult periods."

Do not take criticism personally

- It goes with the job. Remain introspective. Use your insights about yourself to understand your personal reactions to comments made in the media about you and your company. This will help maintain some emotional distance and allow you to respond more objectively.

TWELVE

COMBATING THE ISOLATION OF THE JOB

The participants in the study repeatedly shared how isolating the position of CEO is. Several also described the job as intellectually lonely.

"I don't have anyone to bounce ideas off of. As CEO, people expect me to have figured out the issues before I speak."

"When the company was a lot smaller, I heard Clay Christianson from Harvard describe 'the innovators dilemma.' Everything in that research mirrored what we were experiencing. I heard points of view that were sound that others weren't seeing. It gave me a clearer frame to see the business. I realized it's a lonely intellectual environment. The very folks you choose to promote would create your demise."

"There isn't as much dialogue about and intellectual effort used when making decisions. The environment is so turbulent, there is a greater need for dialogue. Right now, the dialogue isn't deep enough."

"Most people become CEOs because they are successful working for someone, and throughout our careers we have good mentoring, feedback, guidance, and encouragement. As CEO, you will have none of that—and you still need to be successful."

A major factor in CEO isolation is the change in personal and professional relationships when one becomes CEO. Even long-term relationships and friendships are affected, causing the new CEO to feel more isolated than ever. CEOs come to treasure relationships in which people are willing to engage in open, honest conversation. While it is difficult to find people willing to display this candor and discuss issues in an open manner with the CEO, unfiltered input is a critical source of communication and connectedness. It is equally important for the CEO to examine his/her behavior patterns, past or present, that may have contributed to these feelings of isolation. People need to have their heads bitten off only once by a person in power before they will avoid contact with that person. Be sure your behavior as CEO reinforces candor and attacks issues, not people.

> *"Most people become CEOs because they are successful working for someone, and throughout our careers we have good mentoring, feedback, guidance..."*

> *"The minute I was announced as the new CEO, every relationship changed. Everyone wanted to know what I thought or what I wanted before they would say anything."*

> *"As soon as a person is given the title, his/her relationships change, even long-standing relationships, and the nature of communications changes. People become 'afraid' of the CEO and COO for a number of reasons, including the impact they can have over others' careers. As a result, the nature of the information others bring to them changes and the amount of information shrinks."*

12 COMBATING ISOLATION

Study Highlights

The study participants shared that their feelings of isolation in the role fundamentally result from people behaving differently around them and treating them differently once they became CEO. People have multiple reasons why they want something from the CEO, why they treat the CEO like a celebrity, why they read into every nuance of what the CEO says, and why they stop sharing candid information with the CEO. The CEOs generally were surprised by others' reactions; they did not feel they had changed personally when they accepted the job, but clearly others began behaving differently in their presence.

> *"You are 'on' all the time. You are influencing and being influenced all the time."*

The CEOs reported that it was very important to find strategies to deal with the lack of information they received, but needed, in order to be effective. In some cases, they made special efforts to keep the communication channels open within the organization or even to create new communication channels. In addition, they sought advisors without vested interests who would be candid and uncensored. CEOs treasure those relationships, whether they come from inside or outside the organization. The fundamental advice these CEOs offered is to not allow the loneliness/isolation factor to become a self-fulfilling prophecy. They observed that it happens to all CEOs as a function of their role.

The CEOs' experiences and comments are detailed in the following section, in these categories:

1. **People want something from me**
2. **Dealing with "stardom"**
3. **Impact of communicating as the CEO**
4. **Compensating for the lack of candid information**
5. **Advisors**

Detailed Findings

1. People Want Something from Me

CEOs reported that once they accepted the job, people began to treat them as a means to advance their personal agendas. While this occurred when they previously held higher-level positions, it reached a new level when they became CEO.

> *"Once my position was announced, everyone started to treat me differently. For example, people who didn't want to talk to me suddenly were talking to me."*

> *"The number of constituencies I found that I now served expanded significantly, and each constituency has a different set of needs, expectations, and objectives. I found that almost all of the people with whom I came into contact had personal agendas they wanted to promote with and through me."*

> *"You are 'on' all the time. You are influencing and being influenced all the time."*

2. Dealing with "Stardom"

Study participants reported that becoming CEO was a bit like stardom in that their privacy was gone and that people expect you to be 'on' all the time.

> *"I was not prepared for the instant stardom. I refused to be blinded by it or be intimidated by it—but it is there and it is something you have to deal with. I live in NYC, in part, for the anonymity."*

> *"I was also not prepared for the notoriety. I have no anonymity and no privacy whatsoever. I had never experienced anything like that before. Every behavior is being watched. You are paid to always be 'on'—no matter where you are—the day, the time, etc."*

> *"You are a bit of a rock star in this role—and people pay a lot of attention to you in ways that are very different from how they used to."*

3. Impact of Communicating as the CEO

The CEOs reported that their every word is examined and interpreted. Often this is frustrating, because it means that there are very few opportunities for CEOs to explore ideas with others. The CEO might think he/she is testing ideas and casually conversing, but others attribute greater meaning and intent to the CEO's comments and assume they constitute a decision or direction and act accordingly. As a positive, some CEOs recognize that there can be advantages to speaking as the CEO, because their comments carry such weight—a few words can have a significant impact.

> *"If I ask for a glass of water, people give me a reservoir..."*

"Also, every word that I say is examined. If I ask for a glass of water, people give me a reservoir. There are unintended consequences in messages that are sent, especially when they are not clear."

"I have also been surprised by the impact of what I say or do. I found that I have to be careful when I talk because others are likely to magnify my comments or assume that as I think out loud that I am giving them directions. People take me much more seriously than I intend."

"By thinking out loud, I would set the whole organization in motion when I did not intend to."

"I have learned to listen to people and to listen for what they are not telling me. People want to tell me what they think I want to hear and not necessarily what I need to hear. Many times I have to be the devil's advocate and ask 'so, what will happen if we don't do that?'"

"There was a huge advantage of being president, especially with Wall Street."

"On the other hand, the impact of the CEO's comments can be turned into an advantage. For example, I have learned that when I write a personal note to someone about something I think they did well, it carries a great deal of weight with them. Or if I drop in on someone in their office, my visits can have a positive impact. In fact, I have made a habit of sending personal notes to people when I learn of something they have done, and I also send notes to people who are celebrating several years of employment with us."

"People are constantly interpreting my tone of voice, my body language, and the words I use. When I say something, it is likely to be interpreted literally and to be magnified."

"People are constantly interpreting my tone of voice, my body language, and the words I use. When I say something, it is likely to be interpreted literally and to be magnified."

4. Compensating for the Lack of Candid Information

The participating CEOs consistently reported that their normal channels of communication changed as people stopped sharing candid information with them. In response, they make special efforts to seek out information from people throughout the organization, through both formal and informal communication channels.

"Once I became CEO, it was as if I became a different person overnight. It was as if I became a celebrity and whatever I did or said was taken more seriously than before. Furthermore, I no longer get the same level of information about what is going on inside the company like I once did; people are less candid with me. This is true even of some of my older and long-standing relationships. I simply stopped getting the same candor as before. Everyone became instantly less inclined to give me information. I have had to find ways to reach out and get what I consider really useful information. The normal channels do not provide it. I have had to find the few people who will be candid with me. People just seem to be more remote and distance themselves from me."

"Another difference between the roles is that as COO, I was able to 'manage by walking around,' traveling to locations, building personal ties, and asking business-specific questions. Now the travel continues, but my impact is much less tangible and much more symbolic; my presence now is intended to communicate our culture and our values."

"I have to continually work at keeping lines of communication open with the rest of the organization. No one really wants to simply drop in and have an informal conversation, and no one wants to tell me things they think I don't want to hear. Rather, they want to make sure that I hear what they think I want to hear. What I want is to hear what I need to hear, and to hear it on a timely basis. I have tried to do this by having regular meetings with various employee groups, monthly lunches, and periodic travel to our various sites."

---

5. ADVISORS

Many of the CEOs reported that they made special efforts to cultivate advisors—people willing to share their observations and opinions openly. Sometimes these advisors came from within the organization, and sometimes they were from outside.

Outside advisors included consultants, executive coaches, the CEO roundtable, CEO predecessors or other CEOs, and personal friends and family.

"As CEO, I really need someone who is not invested in the job or the CEO title to talk to—someone who can serve as a sounding board and reality check. I have had an executive coach over the past several years who has been immensely helpful in this regard. I also have one longstanding and loyal, but candid, staff member who has been with me a long time. Both of these people are invaluable in that they continue to challenge me and often offer a different perspective."

"Over the years, I have developed a network of trusted advisors in various disciplines. These are people outside the company but whose counsel I value highly..."

"When I needed support, I went outside the company to consultants."

"One thing that surprised me was how alone you are once in the role of CEO. You really have no peers. I have not changed personally, but by the very nature of the role, I no longer had any peers to talk with. As a result, I established a 'kitchen cabinet' that meets three to four times per year to provide an external and unbiased perspective. The kitchen cabinet is an important source of information regarding these activities."

"Externally, I value groups like the CEO 100. It a club of CEOs who get together to talk about pressing topics—we can also acknowledge ideas from one another."

"Over the years, I have developed a network of trusted advisors in various disciplines. These are people outside the company but whose counsel I value highly. These are people who have unique experience and expertise in areas such as law, human resources, etc., and who are not afraid to be candid with me. These are people whose opinions I trust and who have no vested interest in what they say to me."

"My top two key guys and I are willing to share ideas. It's an environment that is safe for us to challenge one another and our ideas."

"I have found a couple of people I can talk to who are outside the management of the company and who I can talk with candidly and freely. I need them to bounce ideas off of and for them to be a sounding board."

"The Business Roundtable is also a chance to toss ideas around . . . It's a great way for a new CEO to hear from a seasoned CEO. 'They put me in that job because they thought I had all the answers . . . but I don't.'"

"I also depended on five people with informal power in the company."

"Additionally, I turned to five CEOs I met in the first quarter."

"AG Lafley and Bob Lane reached out to me. I met with them to discuss what they learned about the early days of being a CEO."

"I have a good business friend from college, and a spouse whom I speak to the most."

Internal advisors are often a handful of very senior leaders close to the CEO, and sometimes they include trusted leaders at other levels. Regardless, they are seen not to have a personal agenda. A number of CEOs commented on the value of a trusted assistant.

"My top two key guys and I are willing to share ideas. It's an environment that is safe for us to challenge one another and our ideas."

"I have lunch with the three operation heads monthly to discuss ideas."

"The CFO, we complement each other. There isn't a decision that I don't run by him."

"I have a close relationship with all past CEOs. I talk with them, and I invite their perspective."

"I also know how treasured peer dialogues are."

"One thing that is invaluable to me in the role of CEO is a trusted assistant. This is someone who can do everything from help me navigate our own internal business processes to help me compensate for my own blind spots. This is also someone who can keep me informed in a candid manner about events and currents throughout the organization. This person can keep me up-to-date on 'news' that otherwise would never be brought to my attention."

"I have a close relationship with all past CEOs. I talk with them, and I invite their perspective."

"Another thing that might have helped in my early years as CEO would have been an executive assistant who could have helped me collect data, process information, offer insights, and convey messages."

Recommendations

Recognize that people will treat you differently now that your title has three new letters in it—CEO. You can expect that people you know well, and some you know less well, will stop sharing as openly and honestly as they did before you became CEO. While they probably do not intend to filter or abridge their comments—though this is how you might feel—the stakes are different for them when they share information with someone who now has the power over their careers, regardless of what a wonderful person they might think you are. Earn their trust by maintaining confidences placed in you and treating confidential information tactfully.

You can expect that some people will see you as a vehicle for advancing their agenda. They see you as someone with the authority and power to make things happen and would like to influence you in ways that make sense to them.

Identify people inside the organization that you trust to give you honest and complete information.

You can expect that people will listen very carefully to everything you say. They will read into your words and inflections, seeking to understand what you want, what you think is important, what they can do to please you. They will take actions that you never intended and might never hear about. They will talk about what you said. They will speculate about what you meant. And you will probably never know about it. If you do hear about it, you will probably be surprised—and disappointed—to learn what you intended to communicate was distorted into something that meant something very different to people.

You will need strategies to assure that your needs for objective information and searching dialogue are met. Many of the sources you have used up to the point of becoming CEO will no longer be available to you.

- Identify people inside the organization whom you trust to give you honest and complete information. Cultivate your relationships with them such that they know how much you value their perspectives and their willingness to provide you with objective information.

- In addition, seek advisors external to the company to stimulate your thinking and provide you with perspectives you would not otherwise get.
  - You might create a "kitchen cabinet" made up of a very small number of both internal people (such as a trusted confidante) and external people (such as a "coach" or trusted consultant) and meet with them regularly and informally.
  - In some cases, you will want experts to prompt your thinking about trends in globalization, technology, energy, etc., that impact your strategic direction. You will want to explore ideas, test out scenarios, and think through options.
  - In some cases, you will want to consult with people who know you and understand the dynamics of your organization well. You will want their advice about how to handle tricky people issues and to run through scenarios about how to deal with your key stakeholders (your Board, your internal advisors, etc.). Consider retaining a high-end executive coach or, if appropriate, your predecessor(s) or close friends with the perspective you need.
  - Find time to "walk around" and meet with people informally in their offices, work locations, or lunchrooms. Demystify the "office of the CEO" by showing your real interest in them and in the part of the business they are involved with.
  - Finally, remember that what you do when you talk with people is important. Even your trusted advisors will be looking to you for "signals" that what they are saying is valuable and being heard. Your comments and your body language can subtly affect what and how much people share with you.

It will also be important to hone how you communicate with people in the organization. No longer will you be able to contemplate an idea out loud in a group of people. You will be expected to be clear in your communications as well as compelling, comfortable, and engaging. You will be expected to know when to listen and when to advocate a point. You will be expected to understand the point of view of the people with whom you are speaking. In short, you will be expected to be "on."

It will be helpful to have a handful of consistent and compelling messages and themes underlying your communications and conversations. These messages will be repeated and tailored to your audiences. You might think that you sound repetitive and uninteresting. You might think that people are waiting for you to say something new. In actuality, people are counting on you to reinforce core values, messages, and strategies.

As the CEOs in the study put it:

> *"The CEO must be relentless and boring in talking about and representing the values, and in talking about what is being done by the company that is consistent with the values."*

> *"I also quickly learned that the vehicles I had used for communicating as COO (such as formal slide decks) were no longer effective. Rather, I found that it was important for me to visit our various locations and to talk with people about their business. In some ways I found this refreshing because these conversations bring me back to the reasons the company exists. As I have done this, I have found new ways to communicate clearly and succinctly. This was a particularly challenging task because of our geographic diversity, the size of our employee population, and the fact that fewer than half of our folks speak English."*

> *"I spend a lot of time out there telling the story of this company."*

It is invaluable to have advisors give you feedback about the impact of your communications. This feedback is critical so that you can hone your messages and learn about how to best connect with different people. They can also tell you if your communications had any unintended impact or triggered any unintended actions.

THIRTEEN

MANAGING THE WORK-LIFE IMBALANCE

The job of CEO is demanding in every sense of the word. It requires physical, mental, and emotional stamina, which often surprised the CEOs.

"I had no idea how physically demanding the job would be. For this job, I need to be energetic, focused, and disciplined."

CEOs are inundated with information, and demands for the CEO's time and attention come from many different sources.

"One thing that has surprised me is the unrelenting demands on my time from different constituencies. This demand comes from employees, the communities in which we operate, investors, and especially the Board members."

"Another surprise for me, also in the area of communications, has been in the amount of information I receive. I am inundated with data and information; it is simply not possible to digest it all. I have had to learn to discipline myself and decide what is really important, and concentrate on those items and to schedule my time accordingly."

"I am expected to know and understand the essential organizational, industry, and environmental issues of various geographies. As CEO and Chairman, I must read and approve everything that is prepared for the Board. I have spent nearly 100 hours reading Board material this week in preparation for the upcoming meeting."

The study participants consistently said that accepting the job had to be a family decision because the job not only impacts the CEO's time and health, it impacts the family as well. In fact, many CEOs rely heavily on time with their families to be the one time and place in their lives in which they can let go of the CEO title and demands and just be a person.

Despite the unrelenting demands, the CEOs in the study consistently said that they enjoyed the job. They recognized it was an honor to be the CEO of their respective companies and they wanted to be successful for all of the people who were impacted by what they said and did. Their rewards don't often come from the personal recognition or from handsome compensation; rather they come from creating something larger than themselves—a great company full of opportunity and rewards for tens of thousands of people, and the opportunity to serve the needs of customers and consumers with their products and services.

"I was not prepared for the pressure and the pace inherent in the role, which is 24/7 and comes from multiple sources, including the Board, regulators, internal staff, NGOs, environmentalists, changing business environment, etc."

"You need to take joy and challenge out of the job other than personal compensation and personal recognition."

"Do not take the job for the money. After awhile, how much money do you need or want? You need to enjoy your accomplishments, but that is not related to your compensation."

"My biggest surprise is that being CEO is as fun as it is."

"I am still learning something interesting most days and a lot on many days and having a great deal of fun at it."

Study Highlights

CEOs described the variety of demands the job places on them and the work-life balance challenges they and their families face as a result. It appears that there may be no such thing as work-life balance, but rather seasons where various life events and factors become the thing that tips the scale (work, family, children, shareholders, analysts, Boards, etc.). Thus, we have come to refer to it simply as "imbalance."

> *"I knew that the job of CEO would be demanding, but I was surprised at how much it truly infringes on my personal life. This is truly a 24/7 job. I find that I must work evenings and weekends, and it can almost be overwhelming."*

> *"Finding a balance as a CEO is a huge challenge. It creates demands on you and on your family that you can't imagine."*

They spoke often about honing their prioritization skills early in their tenure as CEO in order to deal with the unrelenting demands on their time and attention. It is a role full of tradeoffs.

> *"The workload was far beyond what I had expected. The workload is such that it can be difficult to establish priorities as to what receives my attention and what does not."*

> *"I was surprised by the time management and prioritization challenges—both on internal and external things."*

> *"I had to learn to say 'no,' manage my time well/better, and be ever clear about what is important for me to personally spend my time on."*

"Sometimes you have to say 'no' to work; sometimes you have to say 'no' to family. The trade-offs are pretty constant."

The study participants shared many of their strategies for staying balanced. Maintaining their physical well-being through sleep, diet, and exercise is important. In addition, spouses and families provide an important counter-balance to the demands of the job. The CEOs clearly identified their families and time at home as a place just to be a person, not a CEO.

"I don't drink. I stay in shape. I have one job and one wife. I lead a simple life."

"My family has a way of keeping me centered. When I go home, I am not the CEO; I am the person who is told to take out the garbage. My family is very important to me, and understanding the importance of balance in my life helps me understand how important it is to help others manage their work-life balance, as well."

In addition, many of the CEOs commented on how much they value simplicity in their lives. They work to make as much of their lives as simple as possible so that they have the energy and focus their jobs require.

"I don't drink. I stay in shape. I have one job and one wife. I lead a simple life."

The CEOs' experiences and comments are detailed in the following section, in these categories:

1. **Staying connected with family**
2. **The role of the spouse**
3. **Coping with the physical demands of the job**
4. **Personal choices, motivations, and frame of mind**

Detailed Findings

1. Staying Connected with Family

Family was clearly top-of-mind for the study participants. Each of the CEOs described how their families play a critical role in helping them maintain a better work-life balance, often by simply providing them with opportunities to do "regular" things like "regular" people do. Many of the CEOs are married, a few are divorced, a few are single, and many have children. What seems to be more important than marital status is having meaningful, close relationships with family members—children, parents, a spouse—that give them opportunities to shed the responsibilities of CEO and tend to the ordinary, everyday give-and-take inherent in family relationships.

"I coached my children's sports teams throughout their school years and worked hard to stay connected with them."

"I don't have much of a social life. I like to spend time with family every chance I get where I don't have to be 'on.'"

"It relaxes me to do things with my kids and to go to a football game."

"I am very close to my parents, who were very instrumental to the development of my own self-esteem and character-building."

"I love my family, and when they tuck me into bed, I know they love me."

"The kids want only me on the weekends, so when I walk through the door, I leave my title/role at the door and become parent/spouse/ cook/laundry-doer."

"I am divorced and have young kids. When I have my kids, I leave work by four or five p.m. When I don't have my kids, I work like a dog."

"I was prepared for the amount of time the CEO role would require. On the other hand, it required discipline to keep balance in my life. I drove my kids to school every day I was in town. I coached their soccer team. And that is not just me. We try very hard to create a work environment that enables everyone to have work-family balance."

"This is not an eight-to-five job, but family is an important value. I need to set the example by visibly and publicly attending to family events."

"I have been married for 39 years and have two extraordinary kids."

"I have a fiancé and two stepsons."

"My wife and I have been married for 37 years. I have a very strong family life, and this has been really helpful. We have two sons, 25 and 27 years old."

"I was prepared for the amount of time the CEO role would require. On the other hand, it required discipline to keep balance in my life. I drove my kids to school every day I was in town. I coached their soccer team. And that is not just me. We try very hard to create a work environment that enables everyone to have work-family balance."

2. The Role of the Spouse

For married CEOs, the spouse is a confidante, an advisor, a travel companion, and a person who extends the reach of the CEO further than he/she can do alone. He/she often keeps the CEO grounded, providing balance between work and home.

"Because the job requires the CEO's full commitment, including extensive demands on my time, the family must be fully committed as well. The demands on time and attention are far greater than they appear to others. Companies get 'two for the price of one.' For example, we have employees and their families located in third-world countries. It's important for my spouse to travel with me to these locations and be present with the people there."

"Many events and activities include spouses. My spouse has been an extension of me in so many ways."

"My spouse has been an excellent coach to me for 27 years."

"There is a huge sacrifice for the spouse that comes with this job. She goes with me on trips and does a lot to extend the reach I have as CEO."

"My wife has never liked the construct of the CEO's wife."

"My wife is not material in nature and is not 'impressed' by my title or job; she keeps me well-grounded and helps me maintain perspective on the importance of the family."

"Another surprise for me was the stress it put on my personal life. In many ways the spouse becomes an extension of the CEO and this has its positive points, but also has many negative points."

"Your spouse is as important to your career as an executive leader. There is no question in my mind that I would not be a CEO today if I had married someone who was not smart, capable, not secure, not sufficiently independent to be able to get along well when I was away on business. Furthermore, were my spouse not fully committed to our joint life, including our family (three adult children) and this company, I would not have been able to devote most of my waking life to this company."

3. COPING WITH THE PHYSICAL DEMANDS OF THE JOB

The CEOs found their job to be physically demanding and commented on the importance of taking care of themselves.

"The CEO must get regular physical exercise, proper nutrition, and adequate sleep."

"The role of CEO is very taxing and requires long hours and extensive travel. This takes time away from my family and personal life. The support from my strong family has been key. You must be aligned in your values in order for this to work."

"The CEO must get regular physical exercise, proper nutrition, and adequate sleep."

4. Personal Choices, Motivations, and Frame of Mind

Many of the CEOs described personal choices they have made to deal with work-life balance issues. They have made choices about how they think and behave to achieve the balance that works for them.

"Time management with work-life balance is key. I take my full allotment of vacation."

"I don't take calls at home. In 10 years, I have only had five calls."

"The CEO job is all-consuming."

"I need time to think to catch up."

"Carving out time to think is key, but it's so hard and is a very big challenge for me."

"Getting my e-mails doesn't mean I have to answer them right away. My Blackberry is not my boss."

"Anyone who ends up in this job has to be a driver; it shows that they are goal-oriented. They will define balance for themselves. It's a very personal thing. For me, I work 65 to 70 hours a week and travel."

"I am guilt-free about working long days."

"I didn't value work-life balance. However, in the last seven years, I have focused on it."

"I don't do it very well. The CEO job is all-consuming."

"I know this is not something to necessarily talk about, but I find that having a strong tie to my religion is important. I also have observed and believe that it is important for other successful executives. I think it is an important anchor for someone and helps them to be more stable, reliable, and centered."

"I am guilt-free about working long days."

"The person in this role has to be able to laugh at himself/herself. You cannot take yourself too seriously. You are going to make mistakes and you have to have a balance and a sense of humor."

Recommendations

When the demands of the CEO job hit, it is easy to feel as though you have lost control of your time and your life. Anticipate that the demands will be unrelenting, and prepare yourself to take control of your calendar and of your well-being. No one else can do it for you. Remember that this job is a marathon, not a sprint. You will need every ounce of physical, mental, and emotional stamina to succeed as CEO over the long haul.

Here are some of the strategies the study participants recommend:

Commit to Sleeping, Eating Well, and Exercising

- First and foremost, it is important to take care of your physical health. Sleeping, eating, and staying fit are at the top of the list. While you can expect to work long days, travel extensively, and work on your vacations (at least sometimes), it is important to not sacrifice on these basic healthy behaviors.

Get Control of Your Schedule Through Prioritizing How You Spend Your Time

- You will be inundated with information and requests for your time. Every day you will make a series of decisions about what takes priority for you. You will need to make decisions quickly and with less information than you might be comfortable with. You will also need to push decisions down to your leadership team, which makes it all the more important to have confidence in your senior leaders. Every CEO will develop his or her own strategies for prioritization. They have to, because if they don't, the job will bury them.

- It also helps to employ a good assistant. Work with someone who understands your role and empathizes with the demands you are under. You will want someone who represents you well to others when he/she speaks to them on your behalf, particularly when telling them you are unable to talk to them on a moment's notice. Find someone who is confident in making decisions, who has outstanding organizational skills, and who relates well to other people.

Find Time to Put the CEO Title and Role Aside

- You are many things in addition to being CEO—a spouse, a parent, a community member, a friend, a coach, a neighbor. Find time to play those roles, and play them fully, without being distracted by being CEO. Taking time away from the job will enhance your relationships with the people who mean the most to you, and ultimately it will make you a better CEO.

Make Commitments to Your Family

- There will be activities that you probably won't be able to do with your family as you've done them before. However, there are probably a few activities that you—and they—can hold sacred. Talk with your family about the most important commitments, whether it be attending the summer soccer tournament or Saturday movie night, or ordering takeout on Friday. Make those commitments a top priority for connecting with the people who mean the most to you.

Enroll Your Family in Helping You Stay Grounded in What Truly Matters

- Your family loves you. They want you to be healthy and happy. They can help you when you start to get out of balance. They can be your early warning system when you start to get out of balance, and they can help you in ways you probably haven't even thought about. Talk to them about what you are experiencing, and listen to them when they try to help.

Remind Yourself of Why You Took the Job in the First Place

- Chances are that you decided to take the job as CEO to have a positive impact on the lives of many people. Your reward is to create a company, a culture, or a new market, or to provide meaningful employment opportunities for thousands of people. When the job starts to put you into imbalance, take some time to think about why you chose the path you did. What choices do you need to make now to get yourself back into balance so that you can have the impact you set your sights on?

FOURTEEN

Do's and Don'ts for Your Succession

As almost all of the CEOs in the study implicitly or explicitly stated, becoming the CEO involves a transformation in both your professional and personal life. In many ways, the CEOs have been preparing their entire careers, perhaps longer, for the opportunity to become CEO. Among the many learnings from this research are two important findings:

"Behavior matters— not only to your success but to the organization's."

"The first 100 days as CEO are pivotal."

"Behavior matters—not only to your success, but to the organization's."

STUDY HIGHLIGHTS

When many of us think about what it means to be CEO, we think about the awesome responsibility of charting a company's strategic course in light of a rapidly changing world. Interestingly, the study participants consistently said that they felt well-prepared to do that work based on prior experiences and training.

What they offered was unprecedented insight into the areas they felt least well-prepared to handle. Many of the areas in which they felt less well-prepared were actual surprises to them—surprises by their very nature or by their magnitude. Other areas were seen as skill or experience deficits that they quickly identified and began a course of self-development.

In their interviews, they shared what they learned about themselves and how well they fit into the new role. They also shared what they learned about others' expectations for them and what others needed from them.

If any one theme emerged from the study, it was the importance of cultivating and maintaining relationships. Investing the time to understand, communicate with, and demonstrate care and concern for the people around him/her is fundamental to the role of CEO. The Board, the senior team, advisors, and the CEO predecessor are at the heart of the CEO's world and are key to his/her success. The value of healthy relationships with these stakeholders cannot be overstated.

When asked about the biggest derailers a new CEO faces in his/her first two years on the job, one of the study participants answered:
- Relations with the Board
- Relations with the market analysts
- Relations with direct reports
- Complacency about what is in place

The CEOs' recommendations are detailed in the following section, in these categories:
1. Ready, set, lead!
2. Make sure you have prepared for the role
3. Identify and cultivate your networks and advisors
4. Get to know your Board
5. Handle the selection process with grace
6. See the world through the eyes of a CEO
7. Plan the transition with your predecessor
8. Develop relationships with your senior team
9. Assess your leadership team
10. Align your senior team
11. Assess the organization
12. Prepare your family for what the job will mean to you and to them
13. Commit to your own well-being

Recommendations

1. Ready, Set, Lead!

Here is sage advice from one CEO in the study to reflect upon as you get ready to take your seat in the corner office:

"First, quickly put together a description of what 'winning' is and looks like. It is important to remember that in doing so, simplicity is an advantage."

"Second, make sure that you understand the three-to-five strategic planks that will enable the organization to achieve success."

"Third, make sure you have identified and acquired the resources, and established the routines and processes necessary, to enable people to work effectively."

"Finally, make sure you stay the course and do not become distracted from your mission."

"And in the end, it really comes down to respect for people."

---

2. Make Sure You Have Prepared for the Role

While this might sound like an obvious recommendation, it is a helpful way to check for areas where you might either continue your development or compensate for in some other way if any of them is a shortcoming for you.

Career Development Experiences

- **Self-Assessment.** Assess yourself in regard to the personal attributes that other CEOs have identified as integral to the role, and do this in a forthright manner. You might not score high on some of these attributes, but self-candor is critical because it enables you to compensate.

- **Personal Management Practices.** Take stock of the management practices, tools, and models you have developed or adopted during your career, including your decisiveness, and determine if these will continue to be truly effective in fulfilling the accountabilities of the CEO. Often, tools and practices that were effective within a function or at a business unit level are lacking when applied at this level.

- **International Experience.** Live, work, and lead overseas. Experience life as an expatriate where you are "in the minority" in a different culture. Use the experience to refine how you lead people and how you see your business through your customers' eyes. Begin to identify the commonalities of leadership across cultures, and understand the unique aspects of leadership within particular cultures.

- **Board Exposure and Experience.** Sit on one or more Boards, preferably for a for-profit business. Learn Board procedures and how to govern from a Board seat. Learn how to develop sound working relationships with Board members and how to manage what at times might appear to be idiosyncratic Board member behavior.

- **Run a Business.** Take on P&L responsibility. Learn how to balance the competing agendas of different stakeholders and make trade-off decisions in regard to conflicting demands for limited resources to ensure that the organization achieves its desired results.

- **Functional Experience and/or Business Rotations.** Establish a recognized and credible foundational competency in your chosen area of expertise. Learn to appreciate and understand the contributions of other functions and their interrelationships. Learn to lead and orchestrate leaders outside your functional area of expertise.

Secure Resources to Help You Continue to Develop

- Develop one or more relationships with a mentor and/or a coach who will provide you with objective feedback and challenge you to "up your game."

- Engage in continuous learning by seeking development experiences to improve any gaps in your skill sets (e.g., public speaking, analyzing financial statements) and to enhance current strengths.

- Read what the experts are saying in the areas most relevant to you as a leader and to your organization's strategy and customers.

- Participate in and assume leadership roles in industry groups and/or CEO roundtables.

Prepare for and Take Advantage of the Honeymoon Period

- Develop a 100-day plan that considers your key stakeholder groups, what the needs/concerns of those groups are, and how to best connect with them. Map out the key communications points you wish to make—and what questions you will need to ask of them to learn more. Remember to be full of grace and welcoming, especially during these early days. You will want to set a tone of openness where people will want to tell you things they may or may not have had the courage to share with your predecessor.

- Hire a trusted coach, if you do not already have one, to work closely with you behind the scenes through the transition period. He/she can help you develop your plan and be a sounding board as you navigate the early days and weeks and months of the role. He/she should bring experience to help you interpret things you will hear and experience, and serve as an objective sounding board for you, especially during the critical first 100 days.

- Put your thumbprint on the organization. Let people know who you are, what you stand for, and how you are going to lead.

3. Identify and Cultivate Your Networks and Advisors

While it is lonely at the top, you cannot afford to go it alone. It will be important to have people you can turn to inside an outside your organization for perspective, for sharing ideas, for exploring options, and for giving you feedback that you otherwise will not receive. Focus on relationships:

- In industry groups
- In CEO networks—outside your organization and/or by establishing your own advisory group
- With internal leaders—those leaders who you have encouraged to be open and honest with you and who will not be punished for telling you bad news, particularly about yourself
- With an external coach—an objective, skilled coach can be invaluable for providing you with perspective and feedback unavailable anywhere else
- With a trusted assistant who can serve as your alter ego and who can be your eyes and ears in the organization.

4. Get to Know Your Board

- Research the directors individually to know who they are, what their track records are, and what their expectations are.
- Visit one-on-one with each of your Board members in their cities. Bring your spouse, if possible, and get to know their spouses also. Devote the time and energy to developing personal relationships with each director.
- Assess how effectively the Board is working together. Pinpoint improvement areas, and begin working on them. Seek help if needed.
- Pay particular attention to your relationship with the Chairman/Lead Director. Make sure roles and responsibilities are clear and mutually agreed upon. Make the effort to work in concert with the Chairman, even if you disagree on a matter; seek to resolve those disagreements in a mutually acceptable way.

5. Handle the Selection Process with Grace

Throughout the selection process, assume you will be selected as the CEO (however, do not act as though you are entitled). Do this in regard to how you interact with the Board members, other candidates, the predecessor, and members of the senior team. During this period, you are beginning to develop or to redefine relationships. If you are selected to be CEO, your relationships with these constituencies will be instrumental to your success. Don't do or say something during the selection process that burns a bridge you will need once you are CEO. Treat all persons respectfully, and behave as an equal.

6. See the World Through the Eyes of a CEO

There is only one CEO in the company—one person who is the primary face of the enterprise to the external world, one person with the ultimate accountability for the success of the enterprise's strategy, and one person responsible for the orchestration of the organization's component parts. This will require you to elevate yourself from old, comfortable, and previously successful patterns of behaviors.

7. Plan the Transition with Your Predecessor

- Demonstrate sensitivity and support for the outgoing CEO. Give him/her room to make that transition well for him/her. Recognize also, however, that the organization will be looking for your voice, your presence, and your leadership right out of the gate. You must be true to who you are, right from the outset.

- Invest in regular conversations with your predecessor to ensure that both of you get your business and personal needs met during the transition. Recognize that both of you are experiencing significant changes and that communication between you is as important as ever.

- If your predecessor is staying on as Chairman, talk explicitly about how you will work together to fulfill your individual responsibilities on the Board. Remember that as CEO, you are running the company—and you may need to have an explicit conversation that ensures that the outgoing CEO, who may remain on as Chairman, is clear of his/her role change as well. Be mindful of helping to ensure that the public legacy of your predecessor is positive and do everything in your power to support that.

8. DEVELOP RELATIONSHIPS WITH YOUR SENIOR TEAM

- Develop a plan for redefining your relationships with former peers. You will need to be objective about assessing and taking action in regard to their performance, capabilities, values, and potential in ways much different than before.

- If you are leading people who were candidates for the CEO position you now hold, recognize that they will probably be deciding whether or not they will stay with the company. If it is the right thing for them to stay, you will need to go out of your way to tell them privately and demonstrate publicly that you value their talents and contributions, and make your support for them undeniable. This effort on your part can extend to connecting with spouses and family.

- If you are entering the CEO position from outside the company, learn as much about your team as you can before you start the job. Have private conversations with each member to get to know them as people and to learn about their strengths and weaknesses as senior team members. Consider having a skilled facilitator lead a "new leader assimilation" process. Also, consider your senior team's families as extensions of themselves and, to the extent possible, get to know their spouses.

9. Assess Your Leadership Team

- Be clear about your expectations in regard to your vision, your desired future state, your values, and the desired levels of performance, and give everyone a chance to perform. Make sure you are regularly talking with your team about how it's working— what they are accomplishing, and how they are accomplishing it, so there are no surprises between you and the individual team members.

- Fill needed positions early. If you need to create a position to bring needed competency in the organization, do so in a way that prepares the rest of your senior team and the organization to onboard a new person effectively.

- Plan to act on talent issues quickly and fairly by moving people into other positions or out of the organization. Ideally, each person who ultimately leaves the organization will leave with only good things to say about you and about the company.

10. Align Your Senior Team

- You will have a vision for the company and a clear point of view about the strategic direction. If you lack such clarity, you should get help from a strategy consultant or equivalent outside advisor to help lead you and your team through a process to determine what the best strategic direction is for your company. Create communication channels to engage and align the senior team so that they develop ownership of the strategy and can lead its execution.

- Mutually define the behaviors you expect from one another and the commitments you make to each other for leading the company. Provide positive and constructive feedback to your team members about these behaviors. Learn to wear your power lightly. You have the power no matter what, so there is no need to remind others of that power or to be obnoxious in any way.

11. Assess the Organization

- Whether you're inheriting an organization that is performing well or one that is problematic, you will be putting forth new strategies to take the organization into its next chapter. Take stock of how prepared your organization is to execute your strategy and the time it takes for your impact to be felt. This is one of the lessons learned as reported by the CEOs in this study. For example:

"This is not entirely a surprise, but I am amazed at the amount of time it takes to affect change. I know I might be impatient, and I know I can become frustrated, but I would like to see change in our culture occur more quickly. I have talked with my team and everyone seems to understand the need for and to want change but we have to continually struggle with our own inertia; this takes time. People know that we must change but they are not sure what to do differently. They are looking for structure and guidance to help them navigate the process of change."

"There is a cycle time on my communications from when I say things until they are heard and absorbed, and acted upon. You can't change your mind on key messages for 12 to 18 months due to the sheer absorption time of getting your message into and through the organization."

"Defining the new culture was not hard, and I thought it would take only three to five years to get there, but it's going to take more like seven to nine years."

---

12. Prepare Your Family for What the Job Will Mean to You and to Them

- Talk with your family about the job and the new commitments it brings for you. Let them share what they are excited about and what concerns them.

- Identify what your family needs most from you, and discuss how you can work together to make sure you do the things that are most important to all of you.

- Think through what you will need from your family, including keeping you grounded.

13. Commit to Your Own Well-being

- Define what you need to do to maintain your health: sleeping, eating, and exercising.

- Decide whether you need help keeping to your plan, and identify the support you need.

Participating CEOs

We gratefully acknowledge the top corporate leaders who participated in the CEO Study. These dynamic individuals, who often wear the additional hats of Chairman or President, are briefly profiled in the following pages.

Their profiles demonstrate their remarkably varied backgrounds and accomplishments in multiple sectors of global business.

All profiles and portraits were approved by the participants and appear with their express permission. Perspectives are included from two CEOs who requested to remain anonymous. Photos were provided at the option of each CEO.

Once again, we deeply value the CEOs' support and helpfulness in preparing the CEO Study.

PARTICIPATING CEOs

Brad Anderson
Former Vice Chairman & CEO (Retired 2009)
Best Buy Company, Inc.

Best Buy is the largest consumer electronics specialty retailer in the U.S. and Canada, with 17% of the market. Best Buy operates about 1,200 stores in the U.S., Canada, and China, offering electronics, movies, music, computers, and appliances. Founder Richard Schulze opened the first Sound of Music store in St. Paul in 1966, selling audio components. In the early 1980s, the company expanded into video products and appliances, becoming Best Buy in 1983 and publicly traded in 1985. In 1989, Best Buy pioneered a superstore concept that placed all inventory on the sales floor and featured non-commissioned product specialists. In 2001, Best Buy acquired Future Shop, Canada's largest consumer electronics retailer, launching the Best Buy brand in Canada in 2002 and later in China.

Brad Anderson started with Best Buy in 1973 and has been CEO and Vice Chairman since 2002. As CEO, he led the "customer centricity" initiative to create new stores that reflected shopping patterns of local communities. Forbes magazine described customer centricity as "a massive effort to identify and serve the company's most profitable shoppers by rebuilding stores, adding staff, and upgrading wares." In 2004, Forbes named Best Buy company of the year, saying it was boldly "reinventing itself while at the top of its game."

Riley P. Bechtel
Chairman & CEO
Bechtel Corporation

The *Engineering News-Record* has named Bechtel the top U.S. construction contractor for nine consecutive years. The company's diverse portfolio encompasses energy, transportation, communications, mining, oil and gas, and government services.

Privately owned and with headquarters in San Francisco, California, Bechtel has 42,500 employees and offices around the world. In 2007, it had revenues of $27 billion and booked new work valued at $34.1 billion. Bechtel has participated in notable projects such as the construction of Hoover Dam and the cleanup of the Chernobyl nuclear plant. Bechtel's Oil, Gas, & Chemical business unit and Bechtel National, its government contracts group, are its leading revenue producers.

Since 1996, Riley P. Bechtel has been Chairman, CEO, and a Director of Bechtel Group, Inc., which is in its fourth generation of leadership by the Bechtel family. Bechtel received his bachelor's degree in Political Science and Psychology from the University of California at Davis and his J.D. and MBA from Stanford University.

Alan L. Boeckmann
Chairman & CEO
Fluor Corporation

Fluor Corporation is one of the world's largest, publicly owned engineering, procurement, construction, and maintenance services companies. Fluor oversees construction projects for a large range of industrial sectors worldwide while focusing on its core strengths: engineering, procurement, construction, and maintenance. Its projects include designing and building manufacturing facilities, refineries, pharmaceutical facilities, health care buildings, power plants, and telecommunications and transportation infrastructure. Its oil and gas sector accounts for about 50% of sales. Fluor also provides operations and maintenance services for its projects, as well as administrative and support services to the U.S. government.

Alan L. Boeckmann became the Chairman of the Board and CEO of Fluor Corporation in 2002. During his time as the company's President, Boeckmann monitored the changes in his industry related to the growth of the Internet, e-commerce, and the globalization of the workforce. To remain competitive, Boeckmann directed Fluor's investments toward advanced technology and the employee training needed to use that technology effectively.

Richard T. Clark
Chairman, President, & CEO
Merck & Co., Inc.

Merck & Co., Inc. is a global, research-driven pharmaceutical company that discovers, develops, manufactures, and markets medicines and vaccines that address critical, unmet medical needs. Merck is currently one of the largest pharmaceutical companies in the world, both by capital and revenue. Among the biggest sellers are medicines and vaccines that treat ailments such as high cholesterol, hypertension, and diabetes. Some of its well-known pharmaceuticals include allergy and asthma medicine Singulair, cholesterol treatments Zetia and Vytorin, and hypertension fighter Cozaar and Hyzaar.

Company veteran Richard T. Clark was named CEO and President of Merck in 2005, and added the role of Chairman in 2007. He was previously President of Merck's manufacturing division and the Chairman and CEO of Medco Health Solutions. After receiving his B.A. in Liberal Arts from Washington & Jefferson College in 1968, Clark earned his MBA from American University in 1970. In that same year, he served as a lieutenant in the U.S. Army. Clark joined the company in 1972, working his way up from the job of quality control inspector.

Cristóbal I. Conde
Chairman & CEO
SunGard Data Systems, Inc.

With annual revenue of $5 billion, SunGard is a global leader in software and processing solutions for financial services, higher education, and the public sector. Just about every financial services company relies on SunGard Data Systems. A majority of all NASDAQ trades pass through SunGard's investment support systems, which banks, stock exchanges, mutual funds, insurance companies, governments, and others use for transaction processing, asset management, securities and commodities trading, and investment accounting. SunGard provides business continuity, managed information technology, and professional services for businesses that rely on information resources.

After being Chief Operating Officer and a Board member for a year, Cristóbal I. Conde became SunGard's President in 2000, and became CEO in 2002. He was instrumental in taking SunGard private in a leveraged buy-out (LBO) valued at $11.5 billion—at the time, the second largest LBO ever. SunGard is now the largest software company in the world.

Peter A. Darbee
Chairman, President, & CEO
PG&E Corporation

Pacific Gas and Electric Company, incorporated in California in 1905, is one of the largest combination natural gas and electric utilities in the United States. Based in San Francisco, the company is a subsidiary of PG&E Corporation. There are approximately 20,000 employees who carry out Pacific Gas and Electric Company's primary business—the transmission and delivery of energy. The company provides natural gas and electric service to approximately 15 million people throughout a 70,000-square-mile service area in northern and central California.

Peter A. Darbee, a veteran of the energy, telecommunications, and investment banking industries, assumed the role of CEO and President of PG&E Corporation in 2005, and became Chairman of the Board in 2006. Darbee is also a Director of Pacific Gas and Electric Company. Under Darbee's environmental leadership, PG&E Corporation is a founding member of the United States Climate Action Partnership, a group of businesses and leading environmental organizations that have come together to call on the federal government to quickly enact strong national legislation to require significant reductions of greenhouse gas emissions. Darbee has also been active within the energy industry and with state and federal policy makers advocating global climate change.

John V. Faraci
Chairman, President, & CEO
International Paper Company

International Paper is a global paper and packaging company with an extensive North American distribution business. Its primary markets and manufacturing operations are located in North America, Europe, Latin America, Russia, Asia, and North Africa. International Paper (IP) produces uncoated paper, industrial and consumer packaging, and pulp for customers around the world. The company also distributes printing, packaging, graphic arts, and maintenance and industrial products principally through xpedx, its North American distribution business.

John V. Faraci, the company's Chairman and CEO, has held these positions since 2003. He joined the company in 1974 after earning his B.S. in History and Economics from Denison University and his MBA from the University of Michigan. Faraci is a member of the Board of Directors of United Technologies Corp., a member of the Citigroup International Advisory Board, and a Trustee of Denison University. He also serves as a member of the Boards of the Grand Teton National Park Foundation and the National Park Foundation.

Stephen A. Furbacher
Former COO (Retired 2008)
Dynegy, Inc.

Dynegy is a large owner and operator of power plants and a key player in the natural gas liquids business. Dynegy, originally known as Natural Gas Clearinghouse (NGC), was founded in late 1984. The company provides wholesale power, capacity, and ancillary services to utilities, cooperatives, municipalities, and other energy companies in 14 states in key U.S. regions of the Midwest, the Northeast, and the West Coast. The company's power generation portfolio consists of approximately 20,000 megawatts of baseload, intermediate, and peaking power plants fueled by a mix of coal, fuel oil, and natural gas.

Stephen Furbacher served as Dynegy's COO from 2005 until he announced his retirement in late 2007. Furbacher oversaw both Power Generation and Midstream operations and reported directly to Bruce A. Williamson, Chairman and CEO of Dynegy Inc. Furbacher has a bachelor's degree in Mechanical Engineering from Valparaiso University in Indiana.

John H. Hammergren
Chairman, President, & CEO
McKesson Corporation

McKesson Corporation, the largest pharmaceutical distributor in North America, distributes one-third of the medicines used there, supplying prescription and generic drugs and health and beauty care products to retail and institutional pharmacies in the U.S. and Canada. McKesson is also a major medical supply wholesaler and offers software and technical services to providers and insurers to manage supply chain, clinical, administrative, and financial operations.

John H. Hammergren is Chairman, President, and CEO. He joined McKesson in 1996, has been a Director since 1999, and was elected President and CEO in 2001 and Chairman in 2002. He has led McKesson to become the leading provider of supply, information, and care management solutions for reducing cost and improving healthcare quality, more than doubling revenues to $106B, expanding into new markets, and advancing to number 15 on the Fortune 500. McKesson has experienced a cultural transformation driven by establishing core values, committing to continuous process improvement, and using a collaborative approach to customer service.

In 2009, Hammergren became Chairman of the Healthcare Leadership Council, a coalition of chief executives of leading healthcare companies and organizations. He is on the Board of Hewlett-Packard and Nadro, S.A. de C.V. He earned a B.A. in Business Administration from the University of Minnesota and an MBA from Xavier University.

H. Edward Hanway
Former Chairman & CEO (Retired 2009)
CIGNA Corporation

One of the top U.S. health insurers, CIGNA provides coverage for more than 10 million people through its various medical plans. CIGNA also offers specialty health coverage in the form of dental, vision, pharmacy, and behavioral health plans. The company also sells group accident, life, and disability insurance. Its customers include employers, government entities, unions, Medicare recipients, and other individuals in the U.S. and Canada. Internationally, the company sells life, accident, and supplemental health insurance in parts of Asia and the European Union.

H. Edward Hanway was appointed CIGNA Corporation's Chairman and CEO in 2000. Considered by some analysts to be a strong strategist and highly analytical manager, Hanway also has a reputation for instilling a high level of company values. He emphasizes that his view of business is to be a tough competitor, but a competitor with a conscience who plays a vital role in the health and well-being of CIGNA's customers and clients.

Susan M. Ivey
Chairman, President, & CEO
Reynolds American, Inc.

Reynolds American Inc. (RAI) is parent of R.J. Reynolds Tobacco Company, Conwood Company LLC, Santa Fe Natural Tobacco Company Inc., and R.J. Reynolds Global Products, Inc. RAI went public in 2004, following the merger of R.J. Reynolds and Brown & Williamson. In 2006, RAI acquired Conwood, second-largest U.S. smokeless tobacco company. Today, Reynolds American operating companies manufacture and market five of the top ten U.S. cigarettes plus Grizzly, the number-one smokeless tobacco. RAI's Santa Fe produces super-premium cigarettes. British American Tobacco (BAT) holds a 42% interest in RAI.

Susan M. Ivey is Chairman, President, and CEO of Reynolds American Inc., guiding RAI's strategic growth since the merger. Her 27 years in the tobacco industry include a decade of international marketing assignments with BAT. Ivey earned her B.S. from the University of Florida and MBA from Bellarmine College. She serves on the Women's Leadership Initiative for the United Way of America. Board memberships include the Winston-Salem YWCA, Wake Forest University, University of Florida Foundation, Wachovia Forsyth County Advisory Board of Directors, and Salem College for women.

William R. Johnson
Chairman, President, & CEO
H.J. Heinz Company

A premier global food enterprise, H.J. Heinz Company manufactures high-quality branded foods marketed through retail and foodservice. William R. Johnson became Heinz President in 1996, CEO in 1998, and Chairman in 2000. To sustain growth, Johnson transformed the company's global portfolio by divesting $3 billion of non-core assets, adding faster-growing businesses and brands, and refocusing Heinz on three core categories: Ketchup and Sauces, Meals and Snacks, and Infant/Nutrition.

He led Heinz's accelerating growth in emerging markets and championed innovative products. Under his leadership, Heinz drove growth in its Top 15 brands, which generate roughly 70% of company sales. Heinz reported record profit and sales exceeding $10B in FY2009, three-year organic top-line annual growth exceeding 5%, average EPS growth of more than 11%, and operating free cash flow averaging almost 110% of net income. Heinz has delivered dividend growth of almost 56% since FY2004, a compound annual rate of almost 8%.

Under Johnson, Heinz has ranked first in customer satisfaction in food manufacturing for 10 consecutive years. In 2008, PR News selected Johnson as CEO Pioneer of the Year for Corporate Social Responsibility. He is a Director of Emerson, UPS, and the Grocery Manufacturers of America. He was inducted into the Hall of Fame at the University of Texas McCombs School of Business in 2007.

PARTICIPATING CEOs

Donald R. Knauss
Chairman & CEO
The Clorox Company

Clorox offers its namesake household cleaning products, a category in which it is an industry leader worldwide. Its bleach is the cornerstone of the company. Clorox Company, formerly known as the Electro-Alkaline Company, was founded in 1913 by five Oakland, California, investors in order to make bleach using water from salt ponds around San Francisco Bay. Today, Clorox sells products in more than 100 countries and manufactures them in more than 20 countries. Much of Clorox's recent foreign growth has been in Latin America and Canada.

Donald R. Knauss was named Chairman and CEO of Clorox in 2006. He earned his B.A. from Indiana University and served as an officer in the U.S. Marines. He began his business career as a brand manager in the paper products division at Procter & Gamble, and also held leadership positions with the Coca-Cola Company before joining Clorox.

Kenneth D. Lewis
Former Chairman, President, & CEO (Retired 2009)
Bank of America Corporation

The second-largest bank in the U.S. by assets, Bank of America boasts the country's most extensive branch network. Bank of America provides individual consumers, small and middle market businesses, and large corporations with a full range of banking, investing, asset management, and other financial and risk-management products and services. The company serves more than 59 million consumer and small business relationships with more than 6,100 retail banking offices, nearly 18,500 ATMs, and online banking (with nearly 25 million active users). Global Consumer and Small Business Banking, which includes credit cards, is Bank of America's largest segment, and provides deposits, insurance, loans, treasury services, and financing of car, boat, and RV dealerships.

Since 2001, Kenneth D. Lewis has been Bank of America's Chairman, CEO, and President. During his tenure, Bank of America has improved customer satisfaction significantly across every major line of business; annual revenue has increased from $33B to $66B; annual profit has increased from $7.5B to $15B; assets have increased from $642B to $1.7 trillion; market capitalization has grown from $74B to $183B; and total annual shareholder returns (including stock price growth plus dividends) have averaged 13.3%, doubling peers, the KBW Banks Index, the S&P 500, and the Dow Jones Industrial Average over the same period.

Indra K. Nooyi
Chairman & CEO
PepsiCo, Inc.

Indra Nooyi is Chairman and CEO of PepsiCo, which has the world's largest portfolio of billion-dollar food and beverage brands, including 18 different product lines that each generate more than $1 billion in annual retail sales. PepsiCo's main businesses—Frito-Lay, Quaker, Pepsi-Cola, Tropicana, and Gatorade—make hundreds of nourishing foods and beverages that bring joy to consumers in over 200 countries. With more than $43 billion in 2008 revenues, PepsiCo employs 198,000 people worldwide.

Mrs. Nooyi is the chief architect of PepsiCo's multiyear growth strategy, *Performance with Purpose*, which is focused on balancing strong financial returns with giving back to communities worldwide. *Performance with Purpose* is premised on offering a broad array of choices for healthy, convenient, and fun nourishment, reducing environmental impact, and fostering a diverse and inclusive workplace culture. In keeping with this growth strategy, PepsiCo is proud to be listed on the Dow Jones North America Sustainability Index and Dow Jones World Sustainability Index.

Prior to becoming Chairman and CEO, Mrs. Nooyi served PepsiCo in a variety of roles, including President and CFO, Senior Vice President and CFO, and Senior Vice President of Corporate Strategy and Development.

David J. O'Reilly
Former Chairman & CEO (Retired 2009)
Chevron Corporation

Chevron explores for, produces, and transports crude oil and natural gas; refines, markets, and distributes transportation fuels and other energy products; manufactures and sells petrochemical products; generates power and produces geothermal energy; provides energy efficiency solutions; and develops and commercializes the energy resources of the future, including biofuels and other renewables. The company holds interests in 18 fuel refineries and 1 asphalt plant, and it markets gasoline and other products under the Chevron, Texaco, and Caltex brands. Chevron also is a co-owner of Chevron Phillips Chemical Company LLC, one of the world's leading manufacturers of petrochemicals.

David J. O'Reilly has been Chairman of the Board and CEO of Chevron since January 2000. As Chairman and CEO, O'Reilly has led the company through a period of profound growth, resulting in increased production, reserves, assets, market capitalization, and stockholder returns.

James W. Owens
Chairman & CEO (Retiring 2010)
Caterpillar, Inc.

Caterpillar has plants worldwide and sells its equipment globally via a dealer network of 3,600 locations in 180 countries. In addition to making construction and mining machinery, diesel and natural gas engines, and industrial gas turbines, Caterpillar is also a leading services provider through Caterpillar Financial Services, Caterpillar Remanufacturing Services, Caterpillar Logistics Services, and Progress Rail Services.

After joining Caterpillar in 1972 as a corporate economist, Jim Owens held numerous management positions, including assignments in Switzerland and Indonesia. He was elected VP in 1990, named CFO in 1993, elected Group President in 1995, and Chairman & CEO in 2004. He holds a Ph.D. in Economics from North Carolina State University.

Owens is a Director of Alcoa Inc., IBM Corporation, the Peterson Institute for International Economics, the Council on Foreign Relations, and member of the Global Advisory Council to The Conference Board. He is Chairman of the International Trade and Investment Task Force of the Business Roundtable, Chairman of the Business Council, and member of the President's Economic Recovery Advisory Board.

Ronald A. Rittenmeyer
Chairman, President, & CEO (Retired 2008)
EDS Corporation

Electronic Data Systems Corporation (EDS) provides a broad portfolio of business and technology solutions to help its clients worldwide improve their business performance. Its core offerings include information technology, applications and business process services, and information-technology transformation services. A pioneer in the computer outsourcing business, the company delivers services such as systems integration, network and systems operations, data center management, application development, and outsourcing. EDS is one of the largest federal government contractors, but also serves commercial customers in a wide range of industries, including health care, manufacturing, and transportation.

Ronald A. Rittenmeyer has been Chairman, President, and CEO of EDS since 2007. He is responsible for all aspects of EDS' strategy, operations, and execution. Under his leadership, EDS has accelerated its transformation, instilling accountability, increased productivity, and quality at every level of its operations. Rittenmeyer also has enabled $1 billion in cost savings while improving the company's market share and win rates.

Dennis Sadlowski
President & CEO
Siemens Energy & Automation, Inc.

A subsidiary of the German giant Siemens AG, Siemens Energy & Automation (SE&A) manufactures and markets one of the world's broadest ranges of electrical and electronic products, systems, and services to industrial and construction market customers. SE&A, headquartered in the Atlanta suburb of Alpharetta, Georgia, makes products used in the control, distribution, and utilization of electricity. Its technologies range from circuit protection and energy management systems to process control, industrial software, and totally integrated automation solutions. The company also has expertise in systems integration, technical services, and turnkey industrial systems.

Dennis Sadlowski, President and CEO of SE&A since 2007, has executive responsibility for the company's strategic direction, operating performance, and marketplace success. In addition, he is responsible for all staff functions, subsidiaries, and business operations including the sales organization and eight operating divisions: Automation & Motion, Electronic Assembly Systems, Metal Technologies, Postal Automation, Power Conversion, Power Distribution & Controls, Process Solutions, and Residential Products. Sadlowski is also a member of the company's Board of Directors.

Steve Sanger
Former Chairman (Retired 2008)
General Mills Corporation

General Mills markets some of the world's best-loved brands. Its portfolio includes more than 100 leading U.S. brands and numerous category leaders around the world. General Mills is the No. 2 cereal maker in the U.S. and is also a brand leader in flour, baking mixes, dinner mixes, fruit snacks, grain snacks, and yogurt. Its 2001 acquisition of Pillsbury (refrigerated dough products, frozen vegetables) from Diageo doubled the company's size, making General Mills one of the world's largest food companies. Its products are available in 130 countries.

Steve Sanger stepped down in 2007 after more than 12 years as the CEO of General Mills. Sanger continued as Chairman of the company through the end of the 2008 fiscal year in May. Sanger's retirement ended his tenure after a period of strong growth at the Golden Valley-based company. His accomplishments as CEO included doubling sales to more than $12 billion in fiscal 2007 and tripling earnings to more than $1.1 billion. The company also grew its international sales tenfold.

Randall L. Stephenson
Chairman, CEO, & President
AT&T Inc.

A leading innovator and provider of complete communication solutions for consumers and businesses, AT&T Inc. is the world's largest telecommunications company, based on revenue, and in 2009 was named the "World's Most Admired" company in the telecommunications industry by Fortune magazine.

AT&T is a U.S. leader in mobility and broadband. It offers the world's most advanced IP-based business communications services and an award-winning U.S. television service. It is also known as a U.S. leader in local search advertising.

Randall L. Stephenson has been Chairman of the Board, CEO, and President of AT&T Inc. since 2007. As Chairman, Mr. Stephenson has strengthened AT&T's position by focusing on mobility and broadband access to the Internet. Prior to becoming Chairman, he served as the company's COO, with responsibility for all wireless and wired operations. Before that, he held a number of positions with the company or its subsidiaries, including CFO and Senior Vice President—Consumer Marketing. He joined the company in 1982.

David N. Weidman
Chairman & CEO
Celanese Corporation

A global leader in the chemicals industry, Celanese Corporation makes products essential to everyday living. The company's products, found in consumer and industrial applications, are manufactured in North America, Europe, and Asia. Celanese is one of the world's largest producers of acetyl products, which are intermediate chemicals for nearly all major industries, as well as a leading global producer of high-performance engineered polymers that are used in a variety of high-value end-use applications. As an industry leader, the company holds geographically balanced global positions and participates in diversified end-use markets. Celanese operations are primarily located in North America, Europe, and Asia.

David N. Weidman became CEO and President of Celanese Corporation in 2004 and assumed the role of Chairman in 2007. He is also Chairman of the Executive Committee of the American Chemistry Council's Board of Directors and a Board member of the International Council of Chemical Associations. He received his bachelor's degree in Chemical Engineering from Brigham Young University, and his MBA from the University of Michigan.

William Weldon
Chairman & CEO
Johnson & Johnson

Johnson & Johnson has been a part of people's lives for more than 120 years, generating more than 70% of its revenues from No. 1 or No. 2 global leadership positions in its respective markets. Its consistent performance has enabled it to deliver an exceptional track record of growth: 76 consecutive years of sales increases, 25 consecutive years of adjusted earnings increases, and 47 consecutive years of dividend increases. Over the last 10 years, Johnson & Johnson stock generated a 5.6 percent total return for investors compared to a negative 1.4 percent total return for the S&P 500.

In 2002, Bill Weldon became only the sixth Chairman in the history of Johnson & Johnson. In Weldon's first year in his positions, the company recorded a profit of almost $7.2 billion on its sales of almost $41.9 billion. These profits contributed to the continuation of J&J's 70-year trend of increasing revenue each year.

Geoff Wild
President & CEO
Cascade Microtech, Inc.

Cascade Microtech, Inc., is a worldwide leader in the precise electrical measurement and test of integrated circuits (ICs) and other small structures. It delivers access to, and extraction of, electrical data from wafers, ICs, IC packages, circuit boards and modules, MEMS, biological structures, electro-optic devices, and more to technology businesses and scientific institutions that need to evaluate small structures. More than 60% of Cascade's sales come from outside the U.S.

Geoff Wild has been President and CEO of Cascade Microtech since 2008. He holds a B.S. degree in Chemistry from the University of Bath in the United Kingdom. Wild is a member of the Board of Directors for Cascade Microtech, E Ink Corp., and Axcelis Technologies, Inc.

PARTICIPATING CEOs

Patricia Ann Woertz
Chairman, President, & CEO
Archer Daniels Midland Company

 E very day, the 28,000 people of Archer Daniels Midland Company (ADM) turn crops into renewable products that meet the demands of a growing world. At more than 240 processing plants, ADM converts corn, oilseeds, wheat, and cocoa into products for food, animal feed, chemical, and energy uses. The company operates the world's premier crop origination and transportation network, connecting crops and markets in more than 60 countries.

Patricia Ann Woertz joined ADM as CEO and President in 2006, and assumed the additional role of Chairman in 2007, following a successful career in high-level leadership positions. Having worked most of her career in the energy business, she is now leading ADM in expanding its global agricultural sourcing, transportation, and processing operations.

The Researchers
and Authors

Leslie W. Braksick, Ph.D., Cofounder of CLG,
led the research and authorship of this book with
her colleague and veteran C-suite coach James S. Hillgren,
Ph.D., a CLG Partner. They were ably assisted by CLG
Partner and leadership expert Tracy Thurkow, Ph.D.
and CLG consultant and Clinical Psychologist Jennifer
Howard. CLG Senior Consultant Carolina Aguilera,
Ph.D. assembled the confidential biographic and
company data required to support the study. The
following pages introduce these researchers, authors,
and contributors.

Leslie W. Braksick, Ph.D.
Cofounder
The Continuous Learning Group, Inc. (CLG)

Leslie W. Braksick, Ph.D., is a nationally known consultant, executive coach, and author. Her greatest strengths lie in her ability to quickly analyze complex organizational histories and challenging business conditions, while helping her senior executive clients to develop targeted implementation strategies, coach their own leadership teams, and cultivate a culture to achieve strategic change.

Over fifteen years ago, Leslie cofounded The Continuous Learning Group, Inc. (CLG), which is now the largest behaviorally based consulting firm in the world. She has held several pivotal roles in CLG, including Senior Partner, President, CEO, and Chairman, driving CLG's strategy development and execution. Most of Leslie's personal consulting work today is with CEOs and their direct reports and Boards, on matters of executive development and succession, leadership effectiveness, and large-scale change implementation and strategy execution.

The second edition of Leslie's book *Unlock Behavior, Unleash Profits* (2007, McGraw-Hill) ranked #14 on the Wall Street Journal's Best Selling Business Books List in July, 2007. The book has also been ranked #6 of the top 10 business books in 2007 according to 800CEORead. In her book, Leslie makes a compelling case for the critical role that behavior and leadership play in successfully executing business strategy.

Leslie holds a doctorate in Applied Behavior Science and master's in Industrial Psychology. She is currently enrolled at Johns Hopkins University's Bloomberg School of Public Health part-time and expects to complete her MPH in May, 2011.

Leslie is a frequent keynoter or featured speaker at professional conferences. Her recent publications span the topics of executive coaching, behavioral solutions to business problems, and the impact of terrorism on the U.S. economy and business.

Leslie currently serves on the Boards of CLG, Children's Hospital of Pittsburgh and Children's Hospital of Pittsburgh Foundation, Imani Christian Academy, and Princeton Theological Seminary, where she is the Board Vice-Chair.

James S. Hillgren, Ph.D.
Partner and Chief People Officer
The Continuous Learning Group, Inc. (CLG)

James Hillgren, Ph.D., specializes in helping businesses and organizations increase competitive performance by working with executives in the implementation of the unique practices of organizations with sustained high performance. He also provides executive coaching and education to senior leaders in the effective use of behavior-based leadership skills, working with leaders to build appropriate measurement and reward systems that complement and support existing strategy and challenging existing performance measurement systems. He helps leaders guide the development of human performance and reinforcement systems to focus behavior in the right direction.

Jim's experience includes extensive work with clients in organizational redesign, the development of leadership potential, reward and recognition system architecture, and culture change. He has worked with a wide range of industries, including petroleum, manufacturing, civil engineering, telecommunications, healthcare, and insurance.

A graduate of the University of Texas, Jim earned a doctorate in Clinical Psychology. Prior to joining CLG, Jim was national director for Aubrey Daniels and Associates and was a partner with the Hay Group.

He has made presentations to a number of organizations, including the International Association of Business Communicators, the Society for Human Resource Management, the Association for Industrial Engineers and the American Managed Care and Review Association.

Jennifer Howard
Senior Consultant
The Continuous Learning Group, Inc. (CLG)

For over 25 years, Jennifer Howard has consistently assisted clients to improve performance and successfully manage large-scale change. Her focus is on helping clients achieve business results through Executive coaching and development, leadership team effectiveness, creating high-performance organizations, strategy development and deployment, whole-systems architecture and organization design, organizing and implementing customized training programs to assist human resource management become change agents and internal consultants, and integrating change efforts with organizations globally.

Organizations greatly benefit from Jennifer's repertoire of knowledge, skills and experience. Her excellent communication, organizational, and people skills have helped assist all levels of organizations in positive and lasting ways.

Prior to joining CLG, Jennifer cofounded Miller/Howard Consulting Group (acquired by Towers Perrin in 1998), specializing in creating business results through team management and organizational design.

She worked with an international array of businesses in electricity and energy, academia, petroleum companies, restaurants, telecommunications and beverages, in locations such as London, Norway, Denmark, and Puerto Rico.

She has authored articles on creating high-performance organizations and presented at national quality forums. She coauthored *Team Management* and *The Internal Consultant's Guide to Team-Based Organizations*, two workbooks to create high-performance organizations.

Jennifer holds a master's degree in Clinical Psychology from the University of Alabama, and was a child and family therapist before entering management consulting.

Tracy Thurkow, Ph.D.
Partner
The Continuous Learning Group, Inc. (CLG)

Tracy Thurkow, Ph.D., is an expert in working with leaders and internal consultants to create behavior changes associated with large-scale organizational change. Tracy has a reputation for quickly understanding her clients' businesses.

Her clients value her insights and her ability to help them achieve greater personal and organizational success. Over the last 15 years, Tracy has advised executives, project teams, and internal consultants through numerous change initiatives aimed both at business growth as well as at improving operating efficiency, including restructuring, improving the customer experience, and implementing process improvements. Tracy's clients often request her help in charting a roadmap to building a high-performance culture.

Tracy speaks and writes about the role of behavior change in creating large-scale organization change. She has delivered keynote addresses such as "The Push-Pull Dynamic of Culture Change," a practical look at how to create discretionary performance during times of change. A special Six Sigma edition of *Quality Progress Magazine* featured her article, "Minimizing Variability in Six Sigma Implementation—Behavior Is the Key." Her writings on related topics have also been featured in *Pharmaceutical Manufacturing Magazine*.

Tracy holds a doctorate and a master's degree in Industrial/Organizational Psychology with an emphasis in Behavioral Analysis. She has served as an adjunct professor in The American University's Personnel and Human Resources Management Master's Degree Program and as a guest executive instructor at Western Michigan University.

Carolina Aguilera, Ph.D.
Senior Consultant
The Continuous Learning Group, Inc. (CLG)

Carolina Aguilera specializes in working with organizations that are undergoing major change and cultural transformations. Her focus includes leading executive coaching, change leadership, training, and performance improvement initiatives, as well as facilitating high-performance team development and strategic planning sessions. She has also trained internal consultants to build their organizations' change management and change leadership capabilities.

Carolina's recent experience includes leading the implementation of CLG's proprietary *Performance Catalyst*® solution to strategically align and reinforce critical work behaviors to reach the key business results of a Fortune 100 financial services organization. Carolina also worked with the European arm of one of the world's leading consumer-branded companies to improve and integrate their sales and operations planning process. For the same company, Carolina provided change management and change leadership support to executives during the divestiture of two of its businesses. In addition, she has helped organizations from a wide range of industries— including petroleum, healthcare, and pharmaceutical—embed key cultural practices to achieve their business results. Carolina holds both Ph.D. and M.A. degrees in Psychology, with an emphasis in Behavior Analysis. She is fluent in English and Spanish.

Introducing CLG

The Continuous Learning Group, Inc. (CLG), cofounded in 1993 by Drs. Leslie Braksick and Julie Smith, has grown into the largest behaviorally based management consulting firm in the world. CLG's clients come from the Fortune 500—along with non-U.S. clients of similar size.

CLG offers a consulting partnership that has a lifelong impact on its clients, their people, and their organizations. CLG achieves this by applying the science of behavior to clients' most pressing business challenges and opportunities.

Most clients employ one of CLG's three centerline offers, or some combination of them: *Leadership Catalyst*,^{SM} *Performance Catalyst*,® or *Change Catalyst*.^{SM} CLG begins with the client's need and desired outcomes, and then applies world-class talent and tools to help the client navigate successfully through change, while unlocking and unleashing the organization's Discretionary Performance.^{SM}

CLG's consultants work comfortably side-by-side with leaders at all levels, in the trenches, sweating the same details of getting results that the firm's clients do, taking time to build relationships that deliver results.

CLG's work with CEOs and their Boards on issues of CEO succession, executive leadership development, and strategic talent management are heralded by clients who turn to CLG for help in those areas. Similarly, CLG coaches are often found at the BU President and site levels, working with high-potential leaders at all levels to maximize their leadership excellence in areas of greatest importance to the business.

CLG is an enterprise of uncommon people who perform uncommonly well. For a decade and a half, CLG has helped clients achieve remarkable—and measurable—results in ways that also develop sturdy, positive, high-performing cultures. CLG helps execute the behavioral portion of clients' most challenging strategies. CLG helps clients whenever leadership excellence, changing behavior, and emotional engagement are critical to achieving business results.

To discover more, visit www.clg.com or call 800-887-0011 x 2038.

ACKNOWLEDGMENTS

A project like this can be accomplished only with a dedicated team behind it. There are many whose efforts made this possible—to whom we are so grateful—and several deserve specific mention and recognition:

Bill Johnson—without your vision and sponsorship, this project would never have become a reality.

The Participating CEOs—without you, there would be no CEO study and no results to share. Your openness, candor, and trust in our process were gifts to the future leaders of this world, for the next several decades. THANK YOU!

Dana Reinke, Ph.D.—your excellent project management and disciplined editing throughout the entire process were invaluable.

Jamie Berdine—your professionalism, relentless efforts with the staffs of participating companies, creative guidance, and leadership were all key. A vision is only a vision until someone helps it become real. You were the one who helped our vision for the look/feel of the material become a reality. Thank you, thank you!

Carolina Aguilera, Ph.D.—Part IV, the biographies of the participating CEOs, is a tribute to your creative and thorough research on the participating companies and CEOs. Thank you!

Tracy Thurkow, Ph.D. and **Jennifer Howard**—your assistance with the analysis of the findings and helping us turn that analysis into written products was key. Parts II and III reflect your fine handiwork. Thank you!

Ted Smyth—your careful editing and outside-in look at the findings and data interpretations were SO important. Your counsel is always invaluable!

Steve Clark—you were the one to first suggest to Leslie that she ask Bill Johnson "what he wished he knew"—to guide the CEO succession development plans for Heinz. That question gave birth to the whole project!

Fred Schroyer—your editorial assistance and guidance as we converted the Report into this book version were invaluable. Thank you!

Jim Scattaregia—your design of this book is just beautiful.

Barb McGhee—your conscientious management and coordination of work helped make it happen right, as always!

Donna Dotson and **Karen Eonta**—wherever Jim and Leslie were, you two were always on the case. Thanks for all you did throughout.

With tremendous gratitude—
Leslie & Jim

LEADERSHIP
SELF-ASSESSMENT TOOL

To compare your progress against areas felt to be important by our global CEOs, download CLG's exclusive Leadership Self-Assessment Tool (free) at www.clg.com/publications/ceostudy.aspx.

This Leadership Self-Assessment Tool is based on the findings of the CEO Study. It is intended for leaders interested in measuring their own progress toward a corporate senior executive position using criteria defined by our sitting global corporate CEOs.

The CEO Study pointed to distinct leadership attributes, career experiences, and managerial practices reported by the CEOs as being essential to their success. This assessment is aligned with the study's findings and provides an invaluable tool to those aspiring for future global leadership positions.

There are four sections to the Leadership Self-Assessment Tool. The first three align with Parts I, II, and III of this book, and prompt you to think about your performance in specific key areas.

The fourth section is space for you to create your personalized action plan—and put into writing some priority items for you to act on. Your action plan may be to seek feedback about your behavior in key areas. Or it might be to improve in an area you know you need to work on. Or it might be to pursue certain career experiences that you now recognize are important to your preparation and development as a future global executive or CEO. Whatever the steps, they matter because they are important for you.

Don't miss the opportunity to measure your own progress against areas felt to be critically important, by some of the most successful CEOs of our time!

Please turn the page for a snapshot of CLG's Leadership Self-Assessment tool. To receive a copy of the tool, or for assistance, call CLG at 412-269-7240 extension 2038, or email us at **ceostudy@clg.com**.

CLG

Personal Plan

Action Steps

Priority: What will I focus on first?	Goals: What will suc... for me in thi...
1.	
2.	

CLG

Section 4 – Personal Plan

Capture where you are and your priorities as you navigate toward the CEO office. Update your plan as often as useful to you. You can also choose to share the plan with others, particularly a coach or trusted mentor, who can help you achieve your goals.

1 – I was pleased to...

CLG

Section 3 – Managerial Practices

In this section, rate your performance against each of the 9 managerial practices the CEOs identified as foundational to the job. Consider feedback you have received from others, whether from formal performance feedback, a 360° instrument, informal feedback, or a coach. Place a mark in the appropriate column if others have told you that your performance is strong, improving, ... of the qualities, place a mark in the "unclear" column. This is a signal ... ce in this area. Finally, make whatever notes are useful to you in the final did.

...ck I have received, my performance is:			Notes that support my rating:
...mproving	Weak	Unclear	

CLG

Section 2 – Career Experiences

In this section, rate your experience against each of the 9 career experiences the CEOs identified as pivotal. Consider how your performance would be evaluated by others. Place a mark in the appropriate column if your experiences would be considered a success, works in progress, or failures. If you don't have experience in one or more areas, place a mark in the "lacking" column. This is a signal that you need to seek additional experience. Finally, make whatever notes are useful to you in the final column to capture why you rated yourself the way you did.

Experiences pivotal to the readiness and confidence of the CEO:

1. Live and Work Outside the United States Cultivate an awareness and appreciation of other cultures and value for diversity. Create an understanding of the commonalities and differences in effective leadership styles in diverse cultures.

2. Run a Standalone P&L Manage a major integrated organization unit with P&L responsibility. Be in place long enough to own the impact of your decisions and to see how they affect short- and long-term results.

3. Have Strong Foun... Competence, Experi... Whether it's finance, op... marketing, or sales, dev... understanding of various...

4. Lead Frontline O... Develop true understand... for that role, and build... frontline employees.

5. Have Experience ... of the Business Re... complexity of the "eco... up the breadth of the en... action causes another e... powerful reaction.

6. Work with Differe... Constituencies This ... analysts, boards of direc... government regulators, ... leaders.

7. Sit on Other Boa... skills in working with bo... and understand the issue... the dynamics of board-... relations.

8. Learn Through P... skills in managing relati... by leading others, being... protégé, and/or from w...

9. Learn Through C... difficult events with some... Sometimes you will succ... sometimes you will fail.... confidence and continu... success.

CLG

Section 1 – CEO Attributes

In this section, rate your performance against each of the 6 personal qualities the CEOs identified as critical to the job. Consider feedback you have received from others, whether from formal performance feedback, a 360° instrument, informal feedback, or a coach. Place a mark in the appropriate column if others have told you that your performance is strong, improving, or weak. If you don't have feedback about one or more of the qualities, place a mark in the "unclear" column. This is a signal that you need to solicit feedback about your performance in this area. Finally, make whatever notes are useful to you in the final column to capture why you rated yourself the way you did.

CLG

Based on the findings for the CEO Study 2008: What I Wish I Knew

Preparing Leaders for Success
Leadership Self-Assessment

Name: _____

Date: _____

216 LEADERSHIP SELF-ASSESSMENT TOOL